D1716438

Women of Achievement

Georgia O'Keeffe

Women of Achievement

Abigail Adams

Susan B. Anthony

Tyra Banks

Clara Barton

Hillary Rodham Clinton

Marie Curie

Ellen DeGeneres

Diana, Princess of Wales

Helen Keller

Sandra Day O'Connor

Georgia O'Keeffe

Nancy Pelosi

Rachael Ray

Eleanor Roosevelt

Martha Stewart

Venus and Serena Williams

Women of Achievement

Georgia O'Keeffe

ARTIST

Dennis Abrams

CHELSEA HOUSE
PUBLISHERS
An imprint of Infobase Publishing

GEORGIA O'KEEFFE

Chelsea House
An imprint of Infobase Publishing
132 West 31st Street
New York, NY 10001

Library of Congress Cataloging-in-Publication Data
Abrams, Dennis, 1960–
 Georgia O'Keeffe: artist / by Dennis Abrams.
 p. cm. — (Women of achievement)
 Includes bibliographical references and index.
 ISBN 978-1-60413-336-3 (hardcover)
 1. O'Keeffe, Georgia, 1887–1986—Juvenile literature. 2. Painters—United States—Biography—Juvenile literature. I. O'Keeffe, Georgia, 1887–1986. II. Title. III. Series.

 ND237.O5A86 2009
 759.13—dc22
 [B]
                          2008055366

Chelsea House books are available at special discounts when purchased in bulk quantities for businesses, associations, institutions, or sales promotions. Please call our Special Sales Department in New York at (212) 967-8800 or (800) 322-8755.

You can find Chelsea House on the World Wide Web at http://www.chelseahouse.com

Series design by Erik Lindstrom
Cover design by Ben Peterson and Alicia Post

Printed in the United States of America

Bang EJB 10 9 8 7 6 5 4 3 2 1

This book is printed on acid-free paper.

All links and Web addresses were checked and verified to be correct at the time of publication. Because of the dynamic nature of the Web, some addresses and links may have changed since publication and may no longer be valid.

CONTENTS

1   Frustration   7

2   The Early Years   15

3   Student and Teacher   30

4   Finding a Mentor, Lover, and Fame   47

5   Discovering a New Way of Seeing   65

6   Finding Her True Home   83

7   Ghost Ranch   92

8   A Woman on Her Own   102

Chronology   115

Notes   119

Bibliography   125

Further Resources   126

Picture Credits   127

Index   128

About the Author   133

Frustration

The year was 1908. Theodore Roosevelt was the twenty-sixth president of the United States. New York City's Board of Aldermen had just passed the Sullivan Ordinance, which made it illegal for women to smoke in public. (Katie Mulcahey was the first to be arrested under the ordinance before the law was vetoed by the city's mayor.) In Detroit, Michigan, Henry Ford produced his first Model T automobile. Although women did not yet have the right to vote, Mother's Day was observed for the first time, at St. Andrew's Methodist Episcopal Church in Grafton, West Virginia. And, in Williamsburg, Virginia, a young student named Georgia O'Keeffe decided to give up on art school and her dreams of becoming an artist.

The decision was a heartbreaking one for her. For nearly as long as she could remember, all she had wanted to be was an artist. But now it was not to be.

A number of issues forced O'Keeffe to make that decision. One was monetary. Her parents, who had been well-to-do farmers in Wisconsin, had suffered a series of financial losses since moving the family to Williamsburg. Tuition for the Art Students League in New York City, where she had been studying, was now out of the question. Instead, she would have to begin to earn her own living and help her family out as best she could.

There were other factors as well. For anyone to attempt to make a living as an artist, it was (and is) a risky undertaking at best. The world, as they say, is filled with starving artists. For a woman living in the early twentieth century, however, the odds were even more daunting. In 1908, women artists were considered somewhat unusual—art was still something that men made. Women, it was thought, were supposed to fulfill themselves through marriage and family, not through their careers or their art.

And in the unlikely chance a woman did become an artist, there was the question of what kind of artist she could become. While women had been artists throughout history, they were generally relegated to the sidelines of art—and by virtue of traditional notions of the proper role of women, relegated to painting tidy, ladylike portraits or painting inanimate objects, such as flowers and fruit, known as a still life. In such paintings, realism was thought to be the primary goal. The artist strove to paint as *realistic* a picture of the person or object as possible. In the days before photography, painting was the only way a realistic representation of a person, an object, or a landscape could be made.

O'Keeffe, while uncertain of her own path as an artist, rejected realism for realism's sake. "If one could only reproduce nature, why paint at all?" she asked years later. "Rather than spend my life on imitations, I would not paint at all."[1] Of course, this statement was said in hindsight, as O'Keeffe in her later years set about creating her *own* public image, that of a woman who had been determined to become an artist on her own terms or not be an artist at all.

Most likely of course, it was largely financial considerations that kept her out of art school and diverted her away from a career in art. But there was something more. If she *had* to work to earn money, if she couldn't devote herself *wholeheartedly* to her art, she decided that she just wouldn't be an artist at all. A fellow student at the Art Students League said years later:

> O'Keeffe will not admit to personal tragedies, although her face tells a story . . . She only tells you that she had to give up the thing she loved best, painting, in order to fit into the narrow hemmed-in existence which circumstances made for her. Painting remained her passion, but it was all or nothing. Since she could not devote herself to it, she never touched a brush [and] could not bear the smell of turpentine because of the emotions they aroused.[2]

IN HER OWN WORDS

Georgia O'Keeffe did not necessarily get the same pleasure from looking at art as she did by creating it. As she said in a 1971 interview:

> I don't very much enjoy looking at paintings in general. I know too much about them. I take them apart.

A photo of the artist Georgia O'Keeffe taken by Laura Gilpin in 1953. At the time of this portrait, O'Keeffe had come far from her days as an insecure young woman, convinced that she would never paint again.

Can you imagine the pain it would cause you to be forced by circumstance to give up the thing you loved most in life? For three long years, O'Keeffe gave up on her life's dream of becoming an artist. She moved to Chicago, where she found work in advertising. Now her art wasn't a career, it was just a job; one in which she spent the majority of her time drawing lace and embroidery to be used in advertisements for ladies' dresses.

The work was uncreative, uninteresting, and deeply unsatisfying. Friends at the time knew that O'Keeffe was very unhappy, to the point where the unreligious young woman would find herself kneeling in prayer in Catholic churches just to find relief. "There seemed no time to think of anything else, and she didn't want to think about advertising all the time," a friend explained afterwards.[3]

And on top of all that, O'Keeffe, who had grown up in the flat open spaces of the plains before moving to the small-town life of Williamsburg, hated Chicago: hated its crowds, its pollution, and its cold. After two years there, she came down with the measles, which temporarily affected her eyesight, and forced her to return home to Williamsburg, where she discovered that things were worse than ever.

The family's finances were sinking ever lower, and to make matters even worse, her mother, Ida, had contracted tuberculosis and was largely confined to her bed. O'Keeffe was now 23 years old, lacking in education, money, and any prospects for the future. Fortunes, however, were about to change, if not for the O'Keeffe family, then for their oldest daughter, Georgia.

After moving in 1912 from Williamsburg to Charlottesville, Virginia, where her father opened a creamery in a last-ditch effort to save the family's fortunes, Georgia decided to attend a summer school art class with her younger sister, Anita. Anita told her sister that the art professor, Alon Bement, who had recently moved to

Virginia from New York City, had interesting new ideas about art that Georgia needed to hear. O'Keeffe, intrigued, accompanied her sister to the class. What she learned that day opened her eyes to new possibilities in art, stirred her imagination, and gave her the impetus she needed to pick up her brushes again. Once again, she knew that she was going to be an artist, no matter what it took.

Her rise was swift. In just four years, she had her first art show in New York City. In 15 years, she was one of America's most important artists, known for her breathtaking paintings and unique sculptures. In less than 35 years, the Museum of Modern Art in New York was showing a retrospective of her work, the first ever given for a female artist. By the end of her long life, she was a living legend, an icon, known not only for her work, but also for the way she had lived life—alone in the desert, entirely dedicated to her art.

Of course, it is with her paintings that her reputation rests. Whether she was painting larger-than-life flowers in ways never before seen, examining New York City skyscrapers, or invoking the desert with her surprisingly beautiful juxtapositions of animal skulls, flowers, and the sky, her art, her very way of seeing, was unique. Through her art, O'Keeffe made you feel that you were seeing her state of mind. Through her art, she made you feel that you understood her as an artist and as a woman.

The famous American author Joan Didion noted this phenomenon in her essay on O'Keeffe, published in her landmark collection, *The White Album*. In it, Didion describes taking her daughter, then seven years old, to the Chicago Art Institute to see O'Keeffe's enormous *Sky Above Clouds* paintings, done when the artist was in her seventies. Didion's daughter, Quintana, stared at the paintings for a long time, and then turned to her mother, asking her. "'Who drew it,' she whispered. . . . I told her. 'I need to talk to her,' she said finally."[4]

Didion went on to say that:

> My daughter was making, that day in Chicago, an entirely unconscious but quite basic assumption about people and the work they do. She was assuming that the glory she saw in the work reflected a glory in its maker, that the painting was the painter as the poem is the poet, and that every choice made alone—every word chosen or rejected, every brush stroke laid or not laid down—betrayed one's character.[5]

Is it true? Can you judge an artist's character and life by her art? O'Keeffe herself wasn't sure whether it was that important: "Where I was born and where and how I have lived is unimportant. It is what I have done with where I have been that should be of interest."[6]

And while O'Keeffe is in a sense right—that what finally matters is what the artist does, not how he or she lives—it is also true that, through the artist's life, we can come to understand where her art comes from. Through her life, we can greater appreciate what the artist went through to create her art, discover the thought processes that went into the art, and ultimately, learn the ways in which the art does, in fact, reflect the artist. Britta Benke noted in her study of O'Keeffe:

> Georgia O'Keeffe's art was inseparably bound up with her personality. The simple, clear, and poetic character of her painting is equally reflected in her language. It was this oneness with herself that became part of the myth which surrounded her. As her friend [noted photographer] Ansel Adams said of her three years before her death: "She still has a mystique, I call it. It's automatic. She's just

O'Keeffe. She wears a certain kind of clothes, has a certain manner. She's a very great artist. Nobody can look at a painting without being deeply affected. So the mystique begins and endures."[7]

Benke also acknowledged that:

Painting was Georgia O'Keeffe's life, and it was as an artist that she wanted to be understood. Her art echoed her belief in the power and imperishability of nature, a belief which she expressed in countless landscapes and still lifes. . . . Although her pictures at first sight appear easily accessible, they only yield up their true meaning after intense contemplation. O'Keeffe's special predilection for repeating certain patterns, forms, and images and rephrasing them into ever new variations and combinations may be seen as a mark of her efforts to render visible the divine harmony which embraces and connects all things.[8]

By looking at her life and art, we will come to a greater understanding of exactly who Georgia O'Keeffe was. We will see how she grew to become not only America's finest woman artist, but also one of its finest artists, period. We will learn how Georgia O'Keeffe the woman became Georgia O'Keeffe the artist and the legend. As with most legends, the story starts out simply. Hers begins as a young girl growing up on her family's farm in Sun Prairie, Wisconsin.

The Early Years

Born on November 15, 1887, Georgia Totto O'Keeffe was the oldest daughter of Francis Calixtus O'Keeffe and Ida Ten Eyck Totto. Two days after her birth, the announcement that the O'Keeffes had a new child was printed in the local newspaper, the *Sun Prairie Country-man*. While it would be the first time that O'Keeffe's name appeared in print, it would be far from the last.

Like many Americans of her generation, three of her four grandparents were immigrants. On her father's side, the O'Keeffes had come over from Ireland when their family wool business went into decline. After arriving in Milwaukee, Wisconsin, they traveled west to the new settlement of Sun Prairie, where, in July 1848, Pierce O'Keeffe bought land along the Koshkonong Creek for less than a dollar an acre. The land was good, the farm prospered, and his wife, Kate, soon gave birth to four sons: Boniface, Peter, Francis, and Bernard.

Roughly 10 years after the O'Keeffes settled in Sun Prairie, George Victor Totto and his wife, Isabel, bought land adjoining the O'Keeffe farm. George Totto had come to the United States for a completely different reason than the O'Keeffes had; he came in search of liberty and freedom. Once a count in Budapest, Hungary, Totto had fought in a failed Hungarian revolt against Austrian rule. Family legend had it that he was released from jail in exchange for the family's jewels. Whatever the truth of the story, Totto took flight to America, ending up in Sauk City, Wisconsin, where he met Isabel Wyckoff, a 25-year-old orphan who claimed to be a descendant of some of Europe's finest families.

The couple married in 1855, and like the O'Keeffes, started a farm and a family. Isabel had six children, Alletta, Josephine, Charles, Ida, Leonore ("Lola"), and George, in quick succession. The family's farm was successful and was soon larger than that of their more established neighbors. George Totto, though, was unhappy in the United States, and sometime in the 1870s, he went back to Hungary, leaving his wife and family behind. Isabel and her children moved to the nearby college town of Madison in the early 1880s, where she hoped to provide her children with a more civilized existence than she could provide on the farm.

So it was to Madison that Francis O'Keeffe would go to court Ida Ten Eyck Totto. For years, she had been the girl next door, but now Francis, at the age of 30, came to realize that she would make an excellent wife. From Ida's perspective, Francis O'Keeffe was an uneducated farmer, below her in class and status. But O'Keeffe was eager to buy land from the Tottos, so, bowing to family pressure, Ida reluctantly agreed to marry him and returned to the small community she had felt lucky to escape.

To most observers, it seemed a marriage of unequals. As Laurie Lisle notes in her biography of Georgia O'Keeffe, "Throughout their marriage Frank would appear to be in Ida's shadow, even though he was eleven years older than she. People often echoed Ida's early doubts and wondered why a woman who carried herself like an aristocrat had married a humble Irishman."[1]

In any case, Ida O'Keeffe, who at one time had dreamed of becoming a doctor, would have little time to ponder her choice. Within six months of her marriage, she was pregnant with her first child, and for the next eight years, she was either pregnant or tending to a new infant. Seven children would be born in all, including her second child and first daughter, Georgia.

A CHILDHOOD APART

Like many mothers at that time, Ida O'Keeffe was terrified of disease taking away any of her children. The area was rife with stories of entire families being killed by diseases such as diphtheria, typhoid, and smallpox. As one local historian put it, "In return for being a woman and bearing children, the country offered fatal epidemic diseases."[2] The family also had personal reasons for their fears: tuberculosis, an infectious disease of the lungs, had killed all of the men in Francis O'Keeffe's family. So Georgia, born at the beginning of the harsh Wisconsin winter, was safely kept indoors until the spring. One of her earliest memories, she claimed, was of her first time outdoors, sitting on a patchwork quilt with the blue sky above and the green grass coming up around her.

There was another part of this memory as well. Although less than a year old, she said that she was aware that two other children were with her on the quilt, one of them being her older brother, two-year-old Francis Jr., who was Ida's favorite. Georgia said that even then she felt

A sunset over the Wisconsin River. During her childhood in Sun Prairie, Wisconsin, O'Keeffe kept mostly to herself and did not feel a great connection to her family.

neglected in favor of her adorable older brother. "Why doesn't anyone think *I'm* beautiful," she recalled wondering years later.[3] Angry at this neglect, O'Keeffe remembered trying to get off the quilt and being placed back on it in no uncertain terms. It would not be the last time that O'Keeffe would try to assert her independence.

Georgia's parents were a mismatched couple and their styles of parenting were at odds as well. Georgia remembered Francis O'Keeffe as a hardworking, yet easygoing, man who loved to play his fiddle. She was always impressed by her father's "laughter at the things that others took so gravely, of his making light of any little mishap."[4] But he was also a man of action. He was one of the first in Sun Prairie to use mechanical harvesters, and he encouraged his neighbors to permit the installation of telephone lines in the area.

Ida O'Keeffe was just the opposite of the energetic, fun-loving Francis. As biographer Benita Eisler noted, "Ida Totto seems to have been as rigid, retentive, and authoritarian as her husband was permissive, easygoing, and insouciant."[5] Ida, though, was a woman of culture; she played the piano and belonged to a literary club of Sun Prairie women. Ida was eager to pass that culture on to her children. She spent her evenings reading to them, but her choice of reading material tended toward the tastes of her son Francis. Georgia grew up listening to her mother read books like James Fenimore Cooper's *Leatherstocking Tales*, which told the exciting adventures of Natty Bumppo, a white man raised by Native Americans, as well as cowboy and Indian stories that took place in Texas and the New Mexico territory. Music also played an important role in the children's upbringing.

On the other hand, Ida's sense of superiority to the small-town farmers around her had its drawbacks. The O'Keeffe children were allowed to have friends visit at their house but were forbidden to visit their friends' houses in return. Was it fear of illness? Was it fear of what might be learned at the home of her "inferiors?" In either case, Georgia grew used to the high expectations her mother had of her and her siblings but felt she was missing something.

"I think I craved a certain kind of affection that Mama did not give. . . . She counted on us, and we were to do our best as a matter of course because we were her children."[6]

Despite her large family, Georgia kept largely to herself, even at an early age. Not close to her older brother, yet too old to be able to relate to her younger brothers and sisters, Georgia was content to be left alone. By herself, free from the discipline of adults, she was able to explore the land around her. She would sit underneath the family's apple trees, creating an imaginary household using nothing more than clipped grass, weeds, a boat made of a shingle floating in a dishpan lake, and dolls for which she made clothes. Here, she was the ruler of the family, able to exercise her independence and wishes in a way she was unable to at home.

And interestingly, unlike many young girls, she was happy to be alone. She often seemed to stay away from other people, and, as biographer Laurie Lisle pointed out, never needed anyone else to entertain her. "I've never been bored," she said many years later.[7]

Also from an early age, she was inclined to do things her way, to be her own person, to stand out from others. For example, she would only wear white stockings when her sisters were not wearing theirs. "From the time I was a little girl, if my sisters wore their hair braided, I wouldn't wear mine braided," Georgia recalled. "If they wore ribbons, I wouldn't. I'd think they'd look better without it too."[8] Years later, she added, "From the time I was small . . . I was always doing things other people don't do. . . . I was always embarrassing my family."[9]

SCHOOL AND ART

Just before her fifth birthday, Georgia began her formal schooling along with about two dozen other children in the one-room town hall schoolhouse. She was one year younger than the other first graders. (Kindergarten was still a new concept in the United States—the first publicly funded kindergarten opened in St. Louis in 1873.) Although she was the youngest, she quickly showed that she was the equal of anyone in her class.

The years spent listening to her mother read to her had helped, of course. It is also likely that she entered school already knowing how to read; perhaps she learned from one of her aunts, or the school's teacher, who boarded with the O'Keeffes. Remembered as a good student who excelled at schoolyard play, often beating the boys, Georgia attended the school until she was 13 years old.

Along with her daughter receiving a public-school education, Ida was determined that Georgia should learn what every well-raised young woman of her time was supposed to know. First and foremost was the ladylike art of painting. Georgia had always shown an interest in art, and as a young girl she was especially fascinated by the illustrations in her book of Mother Goose nursery rhymes.

Both of Georgia's grandmothers considered themselves artists and painted typical pictures of flowers and fruit in what would today be considered a folk art style. Given the limitations of education in a one-room schoolhouse, art classes were not a part of the curriculum, so Ida O'Keeffe arranged for private art classes for Georgia when she was 12. That winter, Georgia and two of her sisters spent hours practicing the basics of drawing, learning how to copy cubes, squares, and spheres from the assigned drawing book.

By the next year, Ida had decided that the girls needed advanced training and arranged for painting classes from a local amateur painter, Sarah Mann. Mann lived in the village of Sun Prairie, which required a seven-mile round trip in the family buggy every Saturday afternoon, a journey that emphasized to young Georgia the importance that her mother placed on art instruction.

In these classes, Georgia made watercolor copies of illustrations that were supposedly popular with young girls, with subjects like flowers and horses. She was taught to paint as realistically as possible, and her talent as an artist quickly became apparent. She also began to show the traits that she held onto for a lifetime—the desire to draw the best pictures possible, a dislike of being told how to draw, and resentment when someone tried to "fix" her pictures.

Around this time, she came to a startling decision. One day when she was 12, Georgia asked the daughter of the family's washerwoman, Lena, what she wanted to be when she grew up. Lena replied that she did not know. "Well, I'm going to be an artist," Georgia replied.[10] How did she make such a decision, when, in all likelihood, she had never even heard about or seen the work of any female artists outside of her family?

In a book published when she was 90, O'Keeffe described seeing an illustration of a beautiful Grecian maiden in one of her mother's books, a drawing so lovely that it inspired her to want to create something as lovely herself. "I think my feeling wasn't as articulate as that, but I believe that picture started something moving in me that kept on going and has had to do with the everlasting urge that makes me keep on painting."[11]

There was another possible reason, as well. Georgia had always felt that she was somehow outside of her family, the family oddball, someone with "crazy notions." When painting, she discovered that she could be free, with no one to criticize when she used her "crazy notions" in painting colors and shapes. "I decided that the only thing I could do that was nobody else's business was to paint," she said years later. "I could do as I chose because no one would care."[12]

Even as a teenager, O'Keeffe sometimes seemed beyond caring what others thought. She did not grow up thinking that what she could do was limited because of her sex.

Indeed, in one family story, she and her older brother had an argument about whether God was a man or a woman. Georgia insisted that God was a woman, and even when her brother and her mother scoffed at the idea, Georgia refused to change her mind. She was certain, based on the example of strength displayed by her mother and her grandmothers, that God was a woman.

NEW SCHOOL AND OTHER CHANGES

The winter of 1899 was a particularly harsh one in Wisconsin. That February, days after Ida O'Keeffe gave birth to her youngest daughter, Claudia Ruth, the temperature dropped to 34 degrees below zero (-37 degrees Celsius). For Francis O'Keeffe, enough was enough. The fear that he would develop the same tuberculosis that had killed all of his brothers, along with dropping prices for farm goods and an increase in the value of the O'Keeffe farm, led him and his wife to make a decision. It was time to sell the farm and move to Williamsburg, Virginia.

The move, however, would take three years. In the meantime, Georgia was removed from the one-room

IN HER OWN WORDS

Perhaps, too, Georgia O'Keeffe turned to painting as a way to better express herself. She said in 1923:

> I found I could say things with colors and shapes that I couldn't say in any other way—things that I had no words for.

schoolhouse she had attended all her life and transferred to Sacred Heart Academy, a convent boarding school on the outskirts of Madison. There, for the first time, she was forced into a routine without her parents and family, without the family farm, and without the freedom she had always enjoyed.

Instead, she faced a strictly regimented routine. She was only allowed visitors on Saturday afternoons. Teachers were allowed to inspect the students' books and read their mail. And, although as a protestant she was exempt from Catholic religious classes, she was still obligated to wear a black veil for daily chapel and to dress entirely in black on Sundays.

Despite this, Georgia did well in the school's academic program, winning a prize in ancient history. Because her parents were willing to pay extra, she also enrolled in the school's art classes. On her first day of class, she was told to draw a baby's hand from a plaster cast in charcoal. Georgia was pleased with her work, so she was shocked when the nun criticized the drawing as being too small and too black. It was the first time her art had been described so harshly, and Georgia was embarrassed to the point of tears. "I said to myself that I would never have that happen again. I would never, never draw anything too small."[13]

She quickly recovered, and by the end of the school year, her work was displayed in an exhibition. One of her drawings, of a duck hunter aiming his rifle, was published in the school catalog. Along with that, she was given a gold pin "for improvement in illustration and drawing."[14]

It was her first and last year at Sacred Heart, much to her disappointment. The next year, Georgia was taken out of Sacred Heart, and two of her younger sisters were sent in her place. (With only limited funds available, it was thought best to give each of the children at least a "taste" of private school.) Georgia and her brother Francis were sent to live with their mother's sister Lola, a schoolteacher in Madison. The two enrolled in Madison High School, where Georgia did well in her classes and experienced a revelation concerning the possibilities of art.

Until that time, all of Georgia's work had been done copying other people's drawings or plaster casts. Walking past the art class one day, Georgia watched in wonder as the instructor held up a jack-in-the-pulpit plant for the students to examine, showing them the curves and shape of its interior. It was, she said years later, the first time that she realized a drawing or painting could be made of a living thing. Obviously, this had a huge impact on her, and a quarter-century later, O'Keeffe would do a series of six masterful paintings examining that very same type of plant.

The family completed its move from Wisconsin to Virginia in the summer of 1903, leaving the Midwest behind forever. For Georgia, she left her formative years behind as well. She emerged from Wisconsin as a confident, independent young woman who knew what she wanted and was secure in who she was. In later years, she often said that she had "emerged from the soil of the American heartland."[15] It was here where she had developed her passion for wearing black clothes and where she looked back to for inspiration. She often said that the best and healthiest part of her came from her Midwest farm background. "The barn is a very healthy part of me," she wrote years later, discussing her painting of a red Wisconsin barn. "It is my childhood—I seem to be one of the very few people I know of to have no complaints against my first twelve years."[16]

But if her first dozen years were paradise, expulsion from that paradise meant that the next years would be more difficult and painful than any she had experienced.

WILLIAMSBURG, VIRGINIA

When people today think of Williamsburg, Virginia, they see the image of Colonial Williamsburg, the restored historic site of Virginia's colonial capital. When the O'Keeffe family moved there in 1903, however, the restoration had yet to take place. Instead, the family had moved to a city that was, in the words of Laurie Lisle, "a sluggish town of five hundred white and Negro families in which time seemed to have stood still for more than a hundred years."[17]

Williamsburg had little to offer, with the exception of the College of William and Mary. It was home to an inn, a few shops, a pier from which peanuts and watermelons were shipped, and a lunatic asylum. Decay was evident, and the low-lying humid town was subject to yearly epidemics of malaria and typhoid. For many years no direct rail link had existed between Williamsburg and the outside world. For Georgia, this was no surprise, since "there was no earthly reason why anyone would want to go there and no one there had enough money to get away."[18]

The O'Keeffe family had sold the Wisconsin farm for $12,000 and bought a large white home on nine acres in Williamsburg for just $3,500, a house called Wheatlands. Because the family was new to Williamsburg—a tight-knit Southern community that held a distrust of any outsiders, especially Northerners—they would remain outsiders their entire time there.

Unlike the rest of her family, Georgia would spend little time in Williamsburg. While Francis enrolled in the College of William and Mary, Georgia was sent to the Chatham Episcopal Institute, a girls' boarding school 200 miles (322 kilometers) away. Once again, Georgia thrived in the regulated environment, doing well in class and willing to take her punishments when she broke the rules, which was often. As her biographer Benita Eisler points out:

Georgia broke every rule with exuberance: taking unauthorized walks alone or teaching classmates to play poker after 10:00 P.M. curfew, for instance. If she felt the guilt often suffered by the child who escapes an unhappy family, it did not show in the supremely confident, successful student. In her first year at the Sacred Heart Academy, Georgia had learned the first rule of the escape artist: never look back.[19]

She also made a strong impression on her fellow students. She stood out. She looked different from the other girls, as classmate Christine McRae noticed at Georgia's first appearance in evening study hall:

Her features were plain—not ugly, for each one was good, but large and unusual looking. She would have made [a] strikingly handsome boy.[20]

She also dressed differently:

The most unusual thing about her was the absolute plainness of her attire. She wore a tan coat suit, short, severe, and loose, into this room filled with girls with small waists and tight-fitting dresses bedecked in ruffles and bows. Pompadours and ribbons vied with each other in size and elaborateness, but Georgia's hair was drawn smoothly back from her broad, prominent forehead, and she had no bow on her head at all, only one at the bottom of her pigtail to keep it from unplaiting. Nearly every girl in that study hall planned just how she was going to dress Georgia up, but her plans came to naught, for this strongminded girl knew what suited her and would not be changed, though she approved of other girls dressing in frills.[21]

Self-assured and supremely confident, Georgia soon had many of the girls under her spell. If she wanted a classmate to like her, she would set about to do so. Direct and assertive, she had no qualms about her own place in the world, as well as the place of others. "When so few people think at all, isn't it all right for me to think for them and get them to do what I want?" she once asked her friend Christine.[22]

ELIZABETH MAY WILLIS

At Chatham Episcopal Institute, Georgia had the first in a series of art instructors who helped her on her way to becoming an artist. This teacher was Elizabeth May Willis, trained at Syracuse University and the Art Students League. As the school's headmistress and art instructor, Willis was quick to realize that O'Keeffe had considerable talent.

She took Georgia under her wing and gave her the encouragement and freedom to paint as she liked. Georgia could be a difficult student—at times working hard; at other times finding it difficult to do so. When other students complained that Willis did not make Georgia sit at her easel and work, Willis was known to reply that "when the spirit moves Georgia, she can do more in a day than you can do in a week."[23] Willis, who recognized early on that O'Keeffe was a true artist, realized that one could not *force* artists to produce—it has to be done when inspiration and the spirit moves them.

O'Keeffe graduated from Chatham in June 1905. Her fellow students recognized her artistic gifts in the school's yearbook, *Mortarboard*, as "O is for O'Keeffe, an artist divine./Her paintings are perfect and drawings are fine."[24] From Willis, she received a special diploma in art, as well as the art prize for her watercolor painting of red and yellow corn.

She received something else from Willis as well—a strengthened sense of her worth and importance as an artist. As Benita Eisler put it:

> Mrs. Willis's message—that talent enjoyed rights and privileges denied to less-endowed mortals—was thoroughly absorbed by her most gifted student.[25]

Armed with her high school diploma, the 17-year-old O'Keeffe returned home to Williamsburg, to an 18-room house that had yet to be furnished. Francis O'Keeffe, from the proceeds of the sale of the Wisconsin farm, had opened a grocery store, a venture that was the first in what would be a long series of business failures. Staying home was not an option for Georgia, who wanted more than anything to continue to study art. She wanted to get out; the only question was where she would go.

Student
and Teacher

Although it was still considered highly "modern" for parents to send their daughters off to art school, the O'Keeffes, with the encouragement of Elizabeth May Willis, realized that it would be the best move for Georgia. Ida O'Keeffe, in particular, was eager to see her daughter continue her art education. She likely envisioned her daughter becoming, at best, an accomplished art instructor, like Willis. It seems highly unlikely that she could ever have imagined her daughter's ultimate career.

So, Georgia was packed off to Chicago, where she would live in the extra bedroom in the apartment of her mother's unmarried brother and sister. As it still is today, Chicago was the major city in the Midwest, with a population then of nearly 2 million people. Stockyards, factories, and retail interests propelled the city's fortunes. And with fortunes to be made came an elite class eager to be known as art patrons, the builders of the city's great museums.

Georgia enrolled in the art school at the Art Institute of Chicago, one of America's premier fine art museums. In many ways, the school was the wrong choice for her. With its emphasis on traditional techniques and its use of classic European art as the model of what art *should* be, it was hardly the place to encourage the development of American artists like O'Keeffe who were willing to experiment. She would only last a year.

HER FIRST NUDE

For the first time in her life, Georgia was thrown into a booming metropolis, and the institute had a large and diverse student body, most of whom were older and more sophisticated than she was. She felt awkward and out of place, an awkwardness that was accentuated when confronted with her first nude model.

As did all art students, Georgia was required to take a class in anatomy. One day, O'Keeffe was shocked to be confronted with a male model, nude except for just a tiny loincloth. As her instructor pointed out the parts of the model's body, using proper Latin names, she blushed furiously. While she soon grew accustomed to the use of nearly nude models in class, she never quite grew comfortable with the concept as a whole. Throughout her career, she rarely painted the nude body.

There were other difficulties as well. Male students, still hostile to the idea that a woman could even be an artist, often tried to explain to her just why they believed her pictures were inferior to theirs. O'Keeffe also disliked being in the city, disliked the drab classrooms of the art school, and, somewhat surprisingly, was bored and frustrated with the classical sculpture as well as the Old School Dutch and Italian paintings that were at the heart of the museum's collection.

For O'Keeffe, this kind of "classic" art provided little inspiration to her as an artist. These works were far from what she thought art should be, or what she wanted to do as an artist. (It is likely, however, that while in Chicago she saw the exhibition *Hiroshige: Color Prints from the Collection of Frank Lloyd Wright.* This collection of nineteenth-century Japanese woodblocks would have an important influence on her art.)

Despite the difficulties, she still did well in class, and in December she was ranked fifth. By February, she was number one. There was one teacher she did respond to: John Vanderpoel, a hunchbacked Dutchman who emphasized to the aspiring artist the importance of *line* in art, gave her tools and ideas that she could use. He was impressed by her as well, ranking Georgia's drawings first in her class at the end of the school year.

That summer, Georgia returned home to Williamsburg, where she learned firsthand what an unhealthy environment her family had moved to. She developed typhoid fever, an often fatal disease caused by contaminated water or food. Her fever grew so high that she was often delirious, and it seemed unlikely that she would survive. She did recover, of course, although she lost all of her hair as a side effect of the fever and wore a lace cap to cover her baldness.

Still weak from the disease, she was unable to return to Chicago. Instead, O'Keeffe was forced to recuperate in Williamsburg, where she helped to take care of the three youngest children still living at home and cooked for the boarders the family had taken in to make ends meet. By the next summer, O'Keeffe was eager to return to school, but not in Chicago. One factor in her decision may have been a letter of recommendation from the Art Institute, which read in part, "Miss O'Keeffe is a young lady of attractive personality, and I feel that she will be very successful as a teacher of drawing."[1] Obviously, any school that just saw her as a future art teacher was not a school that she wanted to attend.

Another factor played into her decision, too. Her mentor at Chatham, Elizabeth Willis, encouraged her prize student to go to New York City, the nation's art capital, to attend the Art Students League. In New York, she would prove her worth as an artist. It was unusual at the time for a young woman to be allowed the freedom to live alone in a big city, but with her family slowly falling apart around her, O'Keeffe needed to break away. As biographer Benita Eisler pointed out:

> For Georgia, 1907 would be a year of liberation. She had narrowly escaped the year before. And with every mile of the twelve-hour train trip between Williamsburg, the slow dying of her family, the withdrawal of Ida and Francis O'Keeffe into depression, illness, and poverty, was left further behind.[2]

Now nearly 20, Georgia O'Keeffe was prepared for life on her own.

A YEAR IN NEW YORK CITY

Arriving in New York City in September 1907, O'Keeffe was ready to get back to her studies. The Art Students League of New York, founded in 1875, had quickly gained a reputation as one of the nation's finest art schools. There, students from all walks of life could take reasonably priced classes in an informal environment. It seemed—unlike the more formal Art Institute of Chicago—a place where O'Keeffe would be a natural fit.

And she was. Renting a room in a boardinghouse near the school for just a few dollars a week, O'Keeffe quickly became known for her artistic talents, high spirits, and exotic good looks. And while O'Keeffe had always been aloof with men, she met her first serious boyfriend at the Art Students League.

George Dannenberg, a handsome scholarship student from San Francisco, was in O'Keeffe's still-life class, and the pair quickly hit it off, united by a love of dance and the outdoors. Dannenberg escorted O'Keeffe to many school parties, including a Valentine's Day costume party where she dressed as Peter Pan, and a Leap Year dance, where photos show O'Keeffe dressed in a man's dinner jacket and a crooked bowtie, looking into the camera with a distinctly amused look on her face.

Indeed, O'Keeffe, like her father, enjoyed having a busy social life. She loved dancing, music, and conversation. Yet even at a young age, she recognized that those activities were distractions from what truly mattered to her. "I first learned to say no when I stopped dancing. I like to dance very much, but if I danced all night, I couldn't paint for three days."[3]

Her life revolved around her art. Afternoons, O'Keeffe had classes in still life and portraits, taught by the school's most famous art teacher, William Merritt Chase. A respected painter in his own right, Chase had studied art in Europe in the 1870s. His style reflected that of the Dutch and Spanish masters, so much so that he became known as the "American Velázquez."[4] He was a highly sought-after Impressionist portraitist, famous for his paintings of New York City's richest families enjoying their wealth in parks and cafes.

He was known for a teaching system called the Chase Assignment—one oil painting every day. Chase was equally known for his stylish teaching uniform: a silk top hat, suede spats, and gloves, complete with a monocle and a fresh flower in the lapel of his coat. An instructor who believed in encouraging his students, he was, as O'Keeffe later recalled, "fresh and energetic and fierce and exacting . . . and fun!"[5]

She had mixed feelings, though, about his method of requiring one painting a day, each new one to be painted right on top of the previous day's effort: a method designed to help increase the artist's speed and productivity. O'Keeffe later recalled, "Making a painting every day for a year must do something for you,"[6] without exactly specifying *what* exactly it did for her. What she did learn from Chase was a love of color and paint and the importance of being bold with one's choice of colors and textures—lessons that she would use to great advantage as the years progressed.

As much as she loved Chase's classes, O'Keeffe had been forced to sign up for five-month classes instead of eight-month classes to save an extra $30 in her tight budget. Working as an artists' model for other students would have paid her a dollar for four hours of posing, but O'Keeffe resisted as long as she could. She wanted to spend her time

IN HER OWN WORDS

Georgia O'Keeffe also cared deeply for music. According to Laurie Lisle's book, *Portrait of an Artist: A Biography of Georgia O'Keeffe*, O'Keeffe said in 1922:

> Singing has always seemed to me the most perfect means of expression. It is so spontaneous. And after singing, I think the violin. Since I cannot sing, I paint.

doing her own art, not sitting for others. "I wanted to work for myself," she said.[7]

Eventually, she gave in to necessity at the urging of a handsome older student, Eugene Speicher, who would later become a noted portrait artist. It is perhaps evidence of her need for additional income when one learns that Speicher, after O'Keeffe initially turned down his request to be his model, turned to her and said, "It doesn't matter what you do. I'm going to be a great painter and you'll probably end up teaching in some girls' school."[8]

Despite his sneering, contemptuous attitude, O'Keeffe did agree to sit for him, and his portrait of her, entitled *Patsy* (O'Keeffe's nickname at the Art Students League), won the league's $50 Kelly Prize. The portrait shows O'Keeffe gazing straight at the viewer, pale and unsmiling, wearing a plain white blouse with a black bow at her throat. Today, it hangs in an oval frame in the members' room of the League.

In one of those strange coincidences of history, one of the judges who awarded the prize to Speicher was photographer Alfred Stieglitz, who, never having met O'Keeffe, described the portrait as a "swell head."[9] This is the same Alfred Stieglitz who, nine years later, would help O'Keeffe get her first solo art show, the same Alfred Stieglitz who would ultimately become O'Keeffe's mentor, lover, and husband.

By the end of her first year in New York City, O'Keeffe's talents were recognized by her teachers and fellow students. She won the school's top prize of $100 for her painting of a dead rabbit lying next to a copper pot, a painting done faithfully in the style of William Merritt Chase. Despite her success, she was not satisfied.

O'Keeffe was copying the style of others; she still was not doing work that was truly her own. She had done one painting that she felt came close to being what *she* wanted to do: a picture of two poplar trees at night, with the sky

A profile portrait of the photographer Alfred Stieglitz, taken in 1908. His intimate photographs of O'Keeffe would become celebrated in the art world. With O'Keeffe as his muse, Stieglitz in turn became her greatest supporter, and eventually, her husband.

appearing in the space between them. But when she showed the work to another student, he told her that the trees should have been painted differently, and he demonstrated how to do it by painting over her painting with the colors he felt she *should* have used. Despite her anger and frustration,

O'Keeffe began to understand that, for her art to mean anything to her, she would have to paint her way, not the way that others wanted or expected her to.

STARTING AGAIN

It would be, as we learned in the first chapter, another four years before Georgia O'Keeffe picked up a brush again. Forced by financial need, as well as personal frustration and confusion about what she wanted to do as an artist, O'Keeffe worked in Chicago as a commercial illustrator for two years before returning home to Williamsburg, Virginia, in 1910. Two years later, after the O'Keeffes moved to Charlottes-ville, Georgia, she attended summer school art classes with her sister Anita. There, she met the professor who, with one class, inspired her to pick up her brushes again.

His name was Alon Bement. He was a follower of Arthur Wesley Dow, head of the fine arts department at Columbia University's Teachers College, who was known for being a revolutionary in his method of teaching art. As we have seen, most art teachers taught by having their students copy the methods of the great artists of the past or faithfully reproduce inanimate objects. Dow went in a different direction: He taught by freeing his students, by allowing them to master

DID YOU KNOW?

According to an O'Keeffe family legend, while Georgia was working as an illustrator in Chicago, she created the logo used to this day for Little Dutch Girl cleanser. Throughout her life-time, however, O'Keeffe herself would neither confirm nor deny the truth of the story.

the principles of design. His exercises included "dividing a square, working within a circle and enclosing a drawing with a rectangle, then balancing the composition by adding or eliminating elements and changing the placement of masses."[10] Bement, using Dow's methods, encouraged his students to create interesting patterns on their own.

For most students, the Dow method resulted in labored and mediocre work, but for Georgia O'Keeffe, it proved to be a revelation. Reading Dow's textbooks, she learned important lessons on the nature of art and beauty—the principle of abstraction, the idea that lines, forms, and colors can be used to create art without the use of traditional subject matter. She learned his principle of design: "Filling space in a beautiful way."[11] With that, she could put realistic depictions of dead rabbits behind her.

For O'Keeffe, the Dow method gave her the tools and vocabulary she needed to move away from the realistic school of painting that she found so stifling. As Lisle points out, the method provided an alphabet for artists, one that could be used as the artist saw fit, providing the artist the freedom to be an individual. "It seemed equipment to go to work with," O'Keeffe recalled. "Art could be a thing of your own."[12]

The day after meeting Bement, O'Keeffe enrolled in his most advanced class, Drawing IV. Bement was startled and impressed by how quickly O'Keeffe caught on to the technique and by the high quality of the work she did, and gave her a 95 as a final grade. He was so impressed with her work that he asked her to be his teaching assistant the following summer. In the meantime, O'Keeffe needed a winter job. Despite lacking a degree and teaching experience, with Bement's help, she landed a job as drawing supervisor for the Amarillo Public Schools in Texas. O'Keeffe, whose memories of the stories of the Wild West that her mother told her were still fresh in her mind, jumped at the opportunity to leave Charlottesville and her family. "The Wild West, you see. I was beside myself. The openness. The dry landscape. The beauty of that wild world."[13]

As soon as summer school ended that August, 24-year-old Georgia O'Keeffe left for Amarillo. She was eager for new adventure and the chance to see the Texas landscape she had heard and dreamed so much about.

THE WILD WEST

When she arrived in Amarillo in August 1912, the town was still close to its Wild West roots. Its population of 15,000 was made up of small-time merchants, lawyers, hotel operators, prostitutes, and aging cowboys. Saloons outnumbered churches. Living at the Magnolia Hotel, O'Keeffe heard stories about outlaws, cowboys, and frontier justice. Just two weeks after her arrival, she had a story of her own to tell.

One Saturday night, O'Keeffe was in a back room of the hotel playing dominoes with some of the other guests, when she heard three gunshots. Running to the hotel's front door, she witnessed a rancher approaching, a hat pulled down over his eyes, a shotgun still in his hand. A woman asked him what the trouble was; he replied, "Nothing, I've got him."[14] The victim, whose body was lying across the street, was a man who had run off with his wife, the rancher claimed. When the case finally came to trial, the gunman was acquitted after just 10 minutes of jury deliberation.

O'Keeffe fell in love with Texas. "This was my country," she said about her first year there. "Terrible winds and a wonderful emptiness."[15] It was this emptiness that she would respond to for the rest of her life. Laurie Lisle points out in her biography of O'Keeffe:

When she walked to where the wood sidewalks ended at the edge of town, it was as if she were standing on top of the world and seeing the sky for the first time. Day after day its blueness arched above her, with only an occasional white billowy thunderhead racing across it. She could see so far that she was able to detect the approaching weather.[16]

As Amarillo's "supervisor of drawing and penmanship," she was responsible for the art education of hundreds of students in a half-dozen schools. Although O'Keeffe found the job interesting and challenging, using the methods she had learned from Bement sometimes proved difficult. In one exercise, for example, students were asked to arrange maple leaves into seven-inch squares. In Amarillo, though, there *were* no maple leaves, and the few trees that did grow on the dry, wind-blown plain had leaves too small and straggly to be of much use. Still, she tried as best she could, even when she discovered that her students were too poor to bring oranges and flowers to draw for class, and had to fall back on ragweed and rocks. She would do anything she could to get them interested in art. "I'd get them to draw a square and put a door in it somewhere—anything to start them thinking about how to divide a space."[17]

O'Keeffe spent her summers at home in Charlottesville, as Bement's teaching assistant. Since meeting her, Bement had encouraged his young protégé to return to New York City to study with Arthur Wesley Dow at Columbia Teachers College, where Bement also taught for most of the year. For a time, she resisted going back East because she loved Texas. The Texas legislature, however, passed a law requiring the use of textbooks chosen by a state commission, which did not include Dow's textbooks. Exhausted from her battles with the Amarillo authorities to include

Dow's books, O'Keeffe finally tendered her resignation and went back to New York in the summer of 1914.

NEW YORK, PART TWO

The city and its art scene had changed since she had last studied there in 1907. The winter of 1913 had seen the International Exhibition of Modern Art, better known today as the Armory Show, which quickly became known as a watershed moment in the history of modern art. This show introduced New Yorkers, previously only accustomed to realistic art, to the best avant-garde art that Europe and the United States had to offer.

Among the most prominent works was Marcel Duchamp's painting *Nude Descending a Staircase*. In this work, Duchamp, instead of painting a realistic frozen image of a nude woman going down a staircase, actually portrayed the woman's motion by using a succession of superimposed images, similar to a motion picture. While some critics responded in anger to the exhibition, for artists it was a revelation that opened their eyes to other possibilities besides the tradition of realism. The show became a catalyst for American artists nationwide, allowing them to become more independent and willing to create their *own* artistic language.

This environment of new possibilities and new ideas was exactly what O'Keeffe needed. She asked countless questions about the new art, and Dow, far from a traditionalist, was the ideal professor to help her. "There was something insatiable about her—as direct as an arrow and hugely independent,"[18] remembered fellow classmate Anita Pollitzer.

Dow and Bement encouraged their students to experiment, to look at art and the creation of art in new and exciting ways. On one occasion, O'Keeffe walked past Bement's classroom and was fascinated to see the students listening to music being played on a Victrola (a record player) while drawing art to correspond to what they were hearing. O'Keeffe joined the class and created an abstract drawing composed of floating curves, squares, and lines, happy to find a way to combine her love of art with her love of music.

At the same time, though, while modern art was moving toward cubism, which allowed the artist to "break down" or shatter the subject of the painting, Dow encouraged O'Keeffe to move in a different direction. Like him, O'Keeffe was intrigued by Asian art, which appreciated the wholeness of its subject; among European artists she particularly liked the work of Henri Rousseau, who "respected the integrity of natural forms."[19]

O'Keeffe also became increasingly certain about the importance of color in her art, and, as she later confessed, went "color mad" that winter in New York. "Her colors were always the brightest, her palette the cleanest, her brushes the best—although to accomplish this she would do without much else," her friend Anita Pollitzer said later.[20]

When the school term came to an end in the summer of 1915, O'Keeffe, while doing poorly in her teaching classes, excelled in the arts. Dow had nothing but praise for the originality of her painting and drawing. "Miss O'Keeffe is an exceptional person in many ways," he wrote. "She is one of the most talented people in art that we have ever had."[21]

Of course, while living in New York, O'Keeffe took the opportunity to explore the city and see as much new art as possible. She often found herself going with friends to Alfred Stieglitz's 291 gallery. There, on one occasion, after viewing an exhibition of drawings by the artists Georges Braque and Pablo Picasso, she and her friends found themselves being questioned by Stieglitz himself, who asked them about their lives and their reactions to the art. Uncomfortable with people she did not know well, O'Keeffe stepped away from the discussion, to consider her own reaction to the art she had seen. "I didn't understand some of the things he showed, but it was a new wave, I knew that," she later remembered. "It showed you how you could make up your mind about what to paint."[22]

Becoming more and more certain about what she liked in art, she became confident enough to criticize the art done by Dow, who avoided the use of bright colors. "I was liking such snorting things," O'Keeffe wrote in a letter to Pollitzer, "his [pictures] seem so disgustingly tame to me."[23] Upon returning to Charlottesville that summer, she was eager to spread the word about modern art to her students, most of whom were unaware of this emerging style. Her excitement was contagious, and years later many of her students praised her for opening their eyes to what was possible in art.

BREAKTHROUGH

At the end of summer school in Charlottesville, O'Keeffe was faced with a decision. She could either return to New York or take advantage of a new job offer to teach at Columbia College, a school for women in Columbia, South Carolina. She hesitated to take the teaching position. Still, after considering that teaching only four classes a week would allow her ample opportunity for her own painting, she decided to go to Columbia in the fall of 1915.

It was probably a mistake, at least from a teaching standpoint. The campus had suffered a fire in 1910, the college was heavily in debt, enrollment had dropped to just 150 students, and the faculty was tiny. Feeling isolated in a small Southern city, O'Keeffe lived off a steady flow of letters from friends and artists in New York City and refreshed herself with walks through the South Carolina countryside and by filling her room with the flowers she picked.

On the other hand, her small workload, combined with the loneliness of living in a new town, forced her to focus on her art with a greater intensity than ever before. "Hibernating in South Carolina is an experience that I would not advise anyone to miss," she wrote in a letter. "The place is of so little consequence—except for the outdoors—that one has a chance to give one's mind, time, and attention to anything one wishes."[24]

She began to wrestle with the whole idea of art—what did it mean, what was it for, and why did one do it? She knew that she knew the basics of *how* to paint, but what she was not sure of was what painting was for. She also wondered whom she was painting for. Was she painting for herself only, or did she want others to see and enjoy her art?

O'Keeffe came to the conclusion that, in order to proceed, she needed the approval of Stieglitz. The two had still barely spoken, but she knew that he was the most important artist in the country who was actively encouraging the development of a truly American art. She wrote to Pollitzer:

> I believe I would rather have Stieglitz like something—anything I had done—than anyone else I know of—I have always felt that—If I make anything that satisfied me even ever so little—I am going to show it to him to find out if it is any good.[25]

Although she felt the need for Stieglitz's praise, she was still not sure she needed anyone's approval. "I don't see why we ever think of what others think of what we do—no matter who they are—isn't it enough just to express yourself?"[26] It is this tension between the need for approval and the need for self-expression that is a dilemma for many artists.

During this period, O'Keeffe decided to evaluate her standing as an artist. Locking herself in her studio one day that October, she looked carefully at all of her recent drawings and watercolors, noting which ones she did to please a certain professor and which ones were influenced by other artists. As she looked at her work, an idea came to her.

There were abstract images in her mind, personal, intimate, and her own, that she had never had the courage to paint. "This thing that is our own is so close to you, often you never realize it's there," she explained later. "I visualize things very clearly. I could think of a whole string of things I'd like to put down but I'd never thought of doing it because I'd never seen anything like it."[27]

For her, it was a moment of realization and clarity. Although she did not quite yet know how she would get those images from her mind to paper or canvas, she had had her breakthrough. She knew what she wanted to paint.

Finding a Mentor, Lover, and Fame

I grew up pretty much as everybody else grows up and one day . . . [I] found myself saying to myself—I can't live where I want to—I can't go where I want to—I can't do what I want to—. School and things that painters have taught me even keep me from painting as I want to. I decided I was a very stupid fool not to at least paint as I wanted to and say what I wanted to when I painted as that seemed to be the only thing I could do that didn't concern anybody but myself—that was nobody's business but my own.[1]

—Georgia O'Keeffe

After realizing what she needed to do, Georgia O'Keeffe set to work. She put away all of her old artwork. She put away her paint. Not wanting to be distracted by color, she decided to work exclusively in charcoal until she was confident of what she was doing. She was, in effect, starting over. "I had been taught to work like others and after careful thinking I decided that I wasn't going to spend my life doing what had already been done."[2]

She spread sketch paper on her bedroom floor and, crawling over it, worked until her hands were so sore that she could not hold a stick of charcoal. Despite her physical exhaustion, her excitement at what she was doing gave her the energy to continue. For the first time in her artistic life, she was creating the art *she* wanted. "I was alone and singularly free, working into my own, unknown—no one to satisfy but myself."[3]

It was an artistic breakthrough. These drawings were her first truly personal artistic expressions; for the first time her technical abilities were wedded to art that she wanted to create, and the difference was obvious. They were unique, unlike anything else any artist—man or woman—had previously done.

It was perhaps an acknowledgment of how important the drawings were to her that she titled them *Specials*. (For example, one illustration was titled *Charcoal Drawing No. 11/Special*.) Jagged lines and diagonal bars erupt through softer organic shapes—budlike in many cases. Some are reminiscent of volcanoes or at least of an explosion of emotions, with sharp edges rubbing up against soft forms. Laurie Lisle describes them as undulating shapes leaping up like flames reaching for oxygen.

Lisle describes another drawing, labeled *Number Nine*, as showing volcano-like fissures, with fire and steam erupting upward. O'Keeffe visualized this picture while suffering one of the frequent migraine headaches she had during this period.

What the group of drawings did do, for perhaps the first time in history, was to display a truly feminine sensibility.

Three of O'Keeffe's early charcoal works, as seen on display at the National Gallery of Art in Washington, D.C., during a press preview in April 2000. From left are *No. 7 Special*, 1915; *Second, Out of My Head*, 1915; and *No. 2 Special*, 1915.

"The thing seems to express in a way what I wanted it to but—it also seems rather effeminate—it is essentially a woman's feeling—[it] satisfies me in a way," she revealed to her friend Anita Pollitzer.[4] Indeed, the two were so close that O'Keeffe trusted her enough to take a giant leap of faith. She sent a package to Pollitzer in New York that included all of the art she had completed since her breakthrough—with express instructions not to show the works to anyone else.

When Pollitzer opened the package, though, and saw what her friend had accomplished, she knew that she could not keep the drawings to herself:

I was struck by their livingness. Here were sensitive charcoals, on the same kind of paper that all art students were using, and through no trick, no superiority of tools, they were expressing what I felt had not been said in any art I had seen: and what they were expressing seemed important and beautiful. . . . These were rich round forms, in blacks, whites, and grays, beautiful in texture and proportion. . . . I knew after looking at them, in spite of her bidding, that there was one person who must see them. So with the roll of drawings under my arm, I went downtown to 291 and Alfred Stieglitz.[5]

Stieglitz, the man who perhaps knew more about modern art than anyone else in the country, was stunned by O'Keeffe's drawings. "Finally, a woman on paper," was his first response.[6] He went on to tell Pollitzer, "Why, they're generally fine things. You say a woman did these. . . . She's broadminded. She's bigger than most women, but she's got the sensitive emotion—I'd know she was a woman—Look at that line. Are you writing this girl soon? . . . Tell her . . . they're the purest, finest, sincerest things that have entered 291 in a long while. . . . I wouldn't mind showing them."[7]

When Pollitzer returned to her rooms with the charcoal drawings, she wrote to O'Keeffe to tell her what she had done. Pollitzer was very worried that O'Keeffe would be upset that she had shown the drawings to Stieglitz. She need not have worried. O'Keeffe immediately wrote back to thank her for showing her work to the one artist whose opinion she cared about, Alfred Stieglitz. Indeed, it seems likely that O'Keeffe had really wanted her friend to show Stieglitz her work. It seems equally likely that she never would have had the nerve to do so herself.

She did, however, work up the nerve to write Stieglitz, asking him directly what he liked about her pictures. "Mr.

Stieglitz: If you remember for a week why you liked my charcoals . . . I would like to know. . . . I ask because I wonder if I got over to anyone what I wanted to say."[8] Stieglitz, still unaware that he had actually met O'Keeffe on several occasions at his gallery, wrote back:

> What am I to say? It is impossible for me to put into words what I saw and felt in your drawings. . . . I do want to tell you that they gave me much joy. They were a real surprise and above all I felt that they were a genuine expression of yourself. I do not know what you had in mind while doing them. If at all possible I would like to show them, but we will see about that.[9]

As one would expect, O'Keeffe's response was ecstatic. "It just made me ridiculously glad. . . . He must have a pretty fine time living. . . . I just like the inside of him."[10]

ONCE AGAIN TO NEW YORK

O'Keeffe wanted more than anything to go back to New York City, but she had neither the money nor a legitimate reason to go. Fate, however, stepped in. She was offered a new position teaching in Texas that summer, but she needed to take Professor Arthur Wesley Dow's class in teaching methods first. That was all the excuse she needed. She resigned from Columbia College one month into the spring semester.

Once again lacking in funds, O'Keeffe moved into a spare bedroom in the apartment of Anita Pollitzer's uncle, Dr. Sigmund Pollitzer. She quickly settled into the world of school and art, remaining aloof from her landlords, with the exception of their daughter Aline, who was intrigued by O'Keeffe's art and her distinctive looks. O'Keeffe was also dating Arthur Macmahon, a professor of government whom she had met years earlier in Charlottesville, and who, coincidentally, was also Aline Pollitzer's professor at Barnard College.

Bad news from home disrupted O'Keeffe's time in New York City. Her mother's tuberculosis was growing worse. Because of her ill health, she was no longer able to keep their home as a boardinghouse. Georgia's brothers had long since moved out of the house, and her father, whose creamery had failed, was trying to work as a trucker and was gone for long periods of time. Her sister Catherine was studying nursing in Wisconsin. With the exception of her mother's aging sister Jenny, the only ones left at home were Ida, who worked as an art teacher, and Claudia, still in high school.

On May 2, 1916, the O'Keeffes' landlady went to their house, demanding payment of their overdue rent. Ida and Claudia, answering the door, tried to explain that they had no money, but the landlady refused to leave and insisted that their mother come to the door to talk with her. Mrs. O'Keeffe, desperately ill, climbed out of bed and tried to walk down the hall to talk to her, but it was no use. Halfway down the hallway, she collapsed and died from bleeding in her lungs. In the following days, as neighbors who had long avoided the family came to help, they were shocked to learn that the kitchen cupboards were nearly empty. Georgia did not attend the funeral.

FIRST SHOWING

Since returning to New York, O'Keeffe had met Stieglitz on several occasions. She began to think of the older, married man as a mentor, as someone who would help guide her career in the right direction. Still, Stieglitz had a surprise for her. Without her knowledge, he decided to exhibit her work at 291, hanging 10 of her *Specials* along with the work of two male artists.

O'Keeffe knew nothing about the exhibit until one day, while eating in the Teachers College cafeteria, a girl stopped by her table and asked if she was "Virginia O'Keeffe." O'Keeffe naturally replied no, and the girl went on to tell her that *someone* named Virginia O'Keeffe was having an art show at 291. Georgia realized that her art was being shown, and her first reaction was that of dismay. "For me, the drawings were private and the idea of their being hung on the wall for the public to look at was just too much," she recalled many years later.[11]

She immediately went downtown to the gallery, but Stieglitz was away on jury duty. O'Keeffe stayed long enough to note that her work was hung in the larger gallery, while that of the other artists was hung in the smaller ones.

When she returned three days later, Stieglitz was there, and O'Keeffe approached him angrily, asking him, "What right do you have to show these drawings?"[12] She asked that he remove them, but Stieglitz soon calmed her down, telling O'Keeffe that her pictures were so wonderful that he had felt compelled to show them to the public. She asked what he planned to do when the show was over. He promised to take care of the pictures and asked her to send him more as they were done.

The drawings were a small sensation. Word spread throughout New York City's art community that the new drawings on exhibit at 291, done by an unknown woman artist, were something to see. "Miss O'Keeffe's drawings besides their other value were of intense interest from a psychoanalytical point of view," Stieglitz wrote in his magazine *Camera Work*. "'291' had never before seen a woman express herself so frankly on paper."[13] The show, originally intended to run for only a month, was extended.

PSYCHOANALYTICAL POINT OF VIEW?

What exactly did Stieglitz mean when he said that O'Keeffe's work was interesting from a psychoanalytical point of view? At the time of this exhibition, the work of famed Austrian psychoanalyst Sigmund Freud was becoming popular in the United States. Freud, the father of psychoanalysis, had written that one way of looking at art, besides its aesthetic value, was as an expression of the artist's unconscious thoughts or desires.

In O'Keeffe's *Specials* for example, one critic, Willard H. Wright, looked at the jagged lines and soft organic forms and felt that the pictures were really saying that the artist wanted to have a baby. Is that in the drawings? It depends on who is viewing them—what one person sees in a piece of art is often different from what somebody else sees. There is not always a "right" or "wrong" answer to what a picture *means*. For her part, though, O'Keeffe always fought back against such interpretations of her art, certain that critics were trying to say that she was "just" a woman artist.

Regardless of the meaning of O'Keeffe's art, and whether the themes of sexual desire and womanhood were involved, the work and the artist had struck a nerve with critics and audiences alike. "Even many advanced art lovers felt a distinct moral shiver. And, incidentally, it was one of the first great triumphs for abstract art, since everybody got it," noted art critic Henry McBride said.[14]

O'Keeffe, however, had already left the city and missed a great deal of the excitement her work had caused. She was back in Charlottesville, teaching summer school there for the last time and corresponding with Stieglitz, who was quickly becoming more than just a mentor. That August, she left Virginia, eager to go back to her beloved Texas and begin her new job at West Texas State Normal College, in the small town of Canyon.

10 WATERCOLORS MADE FROM THAT STAR

The town was named after Palo Duro Canyon, the second-longest canyon in the United States. It measures roughly 120 miles long (193 kilometers) with an average width of six miles (10 kilometers). It has been called "The Grand Canyon of Texas," referring both to its size and its dramatic geological features, which include multicolored rocks and steep mesa walls. At her first glimpse of the canyon, O'Keeffe was enthralled. "That is something I could paint," she thought,[15] later adding, "It's a burning, seething cauldron, filled with dramatic light and color."[16]

As much as she admired the landscape of Palo Duro Canyon, O'Keeffe was mesmerized more by the general flatness of the land in Texas—prairies that went as far as the eye could see, covered with nothing but limitless blue sky dotted with dramatic cloud formations. It was love at first sight. O'Keeffe relished waking up early in the morning to watch the daily train arrive in Canyon, puffing its way across the flat prairie. Then, as evening came, she would walk west beyond the end of the town to watch the sun drop below the straight line that was the western horizon.

The landscape inspired her. Although Stieglitz had advised her to continue to work in black and white, O'Keeffe began once again to use color. Sparked by the colors of the Texas sunrise, she began to work with the colors needed to capture it, starting with yellows and reds, followed by greens, and before long, she was again painting watercolors using the full color palette. "It is absurd the way I love this country," she said. "I am loving the plains more than ever it seems—and the SKY."[17] She painted it all: the horizons, the canyon, the flat prairie. She even painted four watercolors of houses, carefully examining their lines and shapes.

Her students in Texas had probably never had a teacher like her. She tried to open their eyes to the beauty of the landscape, to teach them the importance of art, and to make them see that art was not just painting pictures, but a way of seeing. "When I taught art, I taught it as the thing everyone has to use."[18] She showed them that they were surrounded by art everywhere they looked, whether it was in the line of a skirt, the way one did one's hair, even one's handwriting. To O'Keeffe, every decision should be affected by one simple consideration—what looked good.

As usual, O'Keeffe had a hard time fitting into the small-town life of Canyon. People did not understand her art. Once, she showed her landlord a picture of sun-colored spheres, which she felt represented her feelings about the canyon. His response? "Well, you must have had a stomachache when you painted it!"[19]

Her long walks alone also struck people as odd, as did the way she dressed. As one student recalled, "We ladies thought she was the queerest dressed person we ever saw—her flat heeled shoes, her black long skirts." Another student added: "She said black made you look small. . . . She wore men's type shoes with low heels and flat soles because she walked with long strides a lot on the prairie and in the canyons."[20]

Early in the school year, O'Keeffe had company on her walks. Claudia O'Keeffe, Georgia's youngest sister, moved to Canyon in October 1916, since their father was on the road and unable to keep an eye on her. The sisters

IN HER OWN WORDS

Georgia O'Keeffe never let being afraid stop her from doing what she wanted to do. As cited on the BrainyQuote Web site, she once said:

> I've been absolutely terrified every moment of my life—
> and I've never let it keep me from doing a single thing I
> wanted to do.

would roam the plains day and night, rifles tucked under their arms.

THE PULL OF NEW YORK

On April 3, 1917, Stieglitz opened O'Keeffe's first solo show at 291. The art included the *Specials* she had done in South Carolina, as well as the more recent Texas landscapes she had completed in Canyon. The positive response was overwhelming. Writing for the *Christian Science Monitor*, Henry Tyrrell remarked:

> [She] has found expression in delicately veiled symbolism for "what every woman knows," but what women heretofore kept to themselves . . . the loneliness and privation which her emotional nature must have suffered put their impress on everything she does. Her strange art affects people variously and some not at all. . . . Now perhaps for the first time in art's history, the style *is* the woman.[21]

For many viewers, the watercolor *Blue Lines* made the strongest impression. Since it was painted with a delicate Japanese brush, it is easy to see how it was influenced by Japanese calligraphy. Initially drawn as two vertical lines in charcoal, O'Keeffe moved on to doing it in black watercolor, before finally settling on the color blue. The picture was interpreted in various ways. Freudians saw the two lines as opposing forces of the mind. Art historians saw them as the contrast between Western and Eastern philosophies. Others, including Stieglitz, saw the two lines as representing the separation between men and women. However the painting was interpreted, it was, by nearly any definition, a memorable work of art.

That show also saw the first sale of an O'Keeffe—a charcoal drawing of a train going around a curve surrounded by a heavy plume of smoke—which sold for $200. News of the sale, combined with her desire to see Stieglitz, propelled O'Keeffe to make a surprise visit to New York just five days after her classes ended and just two weeks before the school's summer session was to begin.

It was a whirlwind visit. Although the exhibition of her paintings had already been dismantled, Stieglitz rehung it for her to see. He also introduced her to other artists he felt she should meet, including one who would have a major influence on her art, photographer Paul Strand. By using extreme close-ups and interesting angles in his photos, Strand made subjects such as chairs, bowls, and fruit appear as abstract shapes rather than as purely realistic objects. O'Keeffe biographer Hunter Drohojowska-Philp points out, "By taking the pictures up close and at dizzying angles, bowl rims, porch shadows, and chair rungs were reduced to pure ovals and angles: his own brand of 'anti-photography.'"[22]

Photographs by Strand, such as *Abstraction, Bowls, Twin Lakes, Conn.*, would prove to have a strong influence on O'Keeffe's art. She approved of the influence of Japanese art in his photos, and through him learned new ways to reach an abstraction of reality. There was more, though, than just an admiration of his art. During O'Keeffe's time in New York, she developed strong feelings for Strand, feelings that he reciprocated. And while she still had feelings for Stieglitz, they were feelings of admiration rather than romance. And, of course, Stieglitz was married, albeit unhappily, to the daughter of a wealthy man who he had been compelled to marry against his will.

In the meantime, O'Keeffe returned to Canyon, not eager to teach, but eager to paint again. She also began a heated correspondence with Strand, in which the pair discussed books, art, and their growing infatuation with each other. In one letter, O'Keeffe emphasized to Strand the influence that his photographs had on her:

> I believe I've even been looking at things and seeing them as I thought you might photograph them—isn't that funny—making Strand photographs for myself in my head. . . . I think you people have made me see—or should I say feel new colors—I cannot say them to you but I think I'm going to make them.[23]

O'Keeffe continued her walks with Claudia, and those evening walks across the flat prairie inspired some of her most colorful and bold watercolors to date, a series called *Evening Star*. Joan Didion described these walks in her essay on O'Keeffe:

> In Texas she had her sister Claudia with her for a while, and in the late afternoons they would walk away from town and toward the horizon and watch the evening star come out. "That evening star fascinated me," she wrote. "It was in some way very exciting to me. My sister had a gun, and as we walked she would throw bottles into the air and shoot as many as she could before they hit the ground. I had nothing but to walk into nowhere and the wide sunset space with the star. Ten watercolors were made from that star."[24]

Looking at Strand's photographs alongside O'Keeffe's painting, it is easy to see the photographer's influence. As Drohojowska-Philp points out, there are stacked circles, similar to the shapes seen in Strand's photographs. There is the same simple composition, the same abstract directness.

The influence of modern photography would become one more component of O'Keeffe's style.

Although she continued to grow as an artist, O'Keeffe was having a difficult time in Canyon. There had been rumors that her relationship with Ted Reid, a 19-year-old college student, was one that was inappropriate between a teacher and a student. In addition, the United States had recently entered World War I, and O'Keeffe's outspoken attitude against the war did little to increase her popularity in town. By the end of October 1917, she was making her unhappiness known in a letter to Strand, "I hate all the folks I see every day—hate the things I see them doing. . . . There is no one here I can talk to—it's all like a bad dream."[25]

Finally, her health broke. It was a harsh winter in Canyon, and O'Keeffe came down with the Spanish flu, an epidemic of which was killing millions of people worldwide. Although she was unable to work, O'Keeffe managed to make the trip to a boardinghouse in Waring, Texas, where the weather was warmer and she could begin a long recovery process.

Stieglitz, a longtime hypochondriac and worrier, was frantic over her condition. He wanted her to come to New York to recover and was hopeful that, in New York, she would fall in love with him. Stieglitz had been infatuated with her for some time, writing letters to her nearly every day. And, while O'Keeffe had tried to keep her relationship with Strand secret from him, Strand and Stieglitz were both well aware of each other's feelings for the talented and beautiful O'Keeffe.

It may seem odd, then, that Stieglitz, desperate to have O'Keeffe near him in New York, gave his romantic rival Strand enough money to take the train to Texas to find out what O'Keeffe's true feelings were, and, if possible, to bring her back to New York. It was obviously a delicate mission.

Strand met O'Keeffe in San Antonio, where they spent several weeks discussing her future. Out of money, weakened from her illness, and uncertain what her future held, O'Keeffe decided to take Stieglitz up on his invitation to come to New York. Arriving there on June 9, 1918, she and Strand were met by Stieglitz, who had arranged for her to live with his niece Elizabeth while she recovered.

O'Keeffe spent the next few weeks in bed, nursed back to health by Stieglitz, his brother Lee, and Elizabeth. Stieglitz, at 54, relished his role as O'Keeffe's caretaker and protector. O'Keeffe, then just 30, appreciated having an older man take care of her, a man who was not only a talented artist himself but who also respected her as an artist in her own right. Soon after O'Keeffe moved into Elizabeth's studio, she and Stieglitz, still unhappily married, became lovers.

SHOWING HIS LOVE

Stieglitz took O'Keeffe to Lake George in the Adirondack mountains, to his family's summer vacation house known as Oaklawn. There, O'Keeffe had the opportunity to meet Stieglitz's large, rambunctious, well-to-do family. Even though Stieglitz was a married man, the family quickly accepted O'Keeffe as the new woman in his life. Indeed, Stieglitz's widowed mother, who had always disliked his wife, Emmy, took to Georgia wholeheartedly. In the words of biographer Laurie Lisle, "As far as she was concerned, her favorite child had fled from a cruel wife into the arms of a young artist with striking grayish-green eyes and beautiful long hands who treated her son affectionately."[26]

O'Keeffe took advantage of the long lazy summer days to paint and to begin to make the transition from watercolors to oils. She felt watercolor was the favored medium of just the kind of women artists she disliked. Oils, the more demanding medium, would help her to elevate her art and allow her to compete on an equal footing with male artists.

And while O'Keeffe recovered from the flu and began to work, Stieglitz was working as well, beginning a new project that would consume him for quite some time. He was creating a full portrait in photographs of the woman he adored, Georgia O'Keeffe.

He had photographed her before, on the occasion of her visit to New York during the summer of 1917. On that occasion, he took pictures of her face and hands, later sending the photos to O'Keeffe in Canyon. "In my excitement at such pictures of myself I took them to school and held them up for my class to see," she said. "They were surprised and astonished too. Nothing like that had come into our world before."[27] In the fall of 1918, in Lake George and upon their return to New York City, Stieglitz began to photograph O'Keeffe in earnest.

"I was photographed with a kind of heat and excitement and in a way wondered what it was all about," O'Keeffe recalled years later upon the publication of some of the photographs.[28] For Stieglitz, photographing O'Keeffe was an act of extraordinary intimacy, claiming, "When I make a photograph, I make love."[29] His goal? "To document the physical and psychological evolution of O'Keeffe's many Selves."[30]

To achieve this goal, Stieglitz took more than 300 photographs of his beloved in less than three years, and nearly 500 in all by the time of his retirement in 1937. To many critics, these photos are among the most extraordinary portraits of an artist and of love in the history of the medium.

He photographed her whole. He photographed her in parts. He photographed her hands, her eyes, her hair, her ears, her neck, her breasts, her stomach, her legs, her feet, her toes, even her most private parts. He photographed her in everyday clothes. He photographed her in men's clothing. He photographed close-ups of her nude body, both standing up and stretched out in bed. He captured her in so many styles, in so many angles, in so many ways, that together, the photos seemed to create a portrait of her as a whole.

O'Keeffe, who did not particularly enjoy posing, did as he requested. It was hard work, because the equipment of the time required that she stay absolutely still for the three to four minutes it took to expose the photographic plates. While she often complained, she was a willing subject, perhaps because she knew that the photos would create an image of her that the public would respond to.

And respond they did. Tired of battling with his landlord, Stieglitz had closed his 291 gallery in June 1917; his next exhibition of photographs, a retrospective look at his career, opened at the Anderson Galleries on February 7, 1921. Nearly one-third of the photographs shown were of a single subject: Georgia O'Keeffe.

The photos caused a sensation. Lewis Mumford said: "Stieglitz achieved the exact visual equivalent of the report of the hand . . . as it travels over the body of the beloved."[31] One young woman began to cry as she stood before the photos. When asked why, she said that the photos showed that Stieglitz "loves her so."[32] Years later, writing in the *New Yorker*, Sanford Schwartz, marveling at the theatricality of the photos, pointed out that "in these pictures, O'Keeffe is the one great actress of still photography."[33]

O'Keeffe went from being a virtual unknown to the talk of the New York art world. Critic Henry McBride wrote in the *New York Sun*:

> There came to notice almost at once . . . some photographs showing every conceivable aspect of O'Keeffe that was a new effort in photography and something new in the way of introducing a budding artist. It made a stir. Mona Lisa got but one portrait of herself worth talking about. O'Keeffe got a

hundred. It put her at once on the map. Everybody knew the name. She became what is known as a newspaper personality.[34]

From Stieglitz's perspective the show had gone even better than expected. His photographs were acclaimed as being his best in years, and through them, he had helped introduce his lover to the New York art world. There was one problem, however. O'Keeffe was not very happy about the exhibition or becoming a "newspaper personality."

Discovering a
New Way of Seeing

Georgia O'Keeffe had thought of Alfred Stieglitz's photographs as impersonal works of art and was dismayed when critics and viewers alike saw and interpreted them in the most personal terms. Stieglitz, by displaying intimate, clothed, and partially nude photographs of O'Keeffe (at the pleading of his family, he decided against showing the most intimate photos), had declared, in a most public way, his love for O'Keeffe.

For her part, O'Keeffe was humiliated by the showing, which she felt displayed her as nothing more than Stieglitz's mistress. "I almost wept," she said. "I thought I could never face the world again."[1] O'Keeffe wanted to be seen not just as the girlfriend of the great Alfred Stieglitz, but as an artist in her own right.

She had, of course, been painting on her own during the three years that Stieglitz was most actively photographing her. Her work during this time reflected her happiness and contentment with the relationship. These new works also displayed her continued use of oil, as well as the influence of artist Stanton MacDonald-Wright and his theories of synchromism—a concept that color and sound are very similar phenomena. So, in the same way that a composer arranges notes in a symphony, an artist can orchestrate the colors in a painting to blend in the same harmonious way. O'Keeffe, who had always been interested in ways to combine her love of music and art, was instantly attracted to the idea.

This can be seen in three paintings that she did in 1919: *Blue and Green Music*, as well as *Music—Pink and Blue*, (I and II). MacDonald-Wright used muted tones in his works, which showed dark tunnels. O'Keeffe, especially in the two *Music—Pink and Blue* paintings, changed the dark tunnel to shades of pink and white, creating a tunnel that opens up to a bright blue color at its end. (This bright blue would reappear years later in her famous Pelvis and Sky series of the mid-1940s.)

Her artwork also reflected her longing for Texas. In her painting *Red and Orange Streak*, also from 1919, O'Keeffe shows a landscape of a dark field and sky that is cut nearly in half at the horizon line by a "chain of blood-colored mountains. A sickle of gold rises up in the work, an apparition generated by memories of the haunting sound of cattle in their pens lowing for their calves. 'It had a regular rhythmic beat . . . repeating the same rhythms over and over all through the day and night,' she later recalled. 'It was loud and raw under the stars in that wide empty country.'"[2]

Her work continued to grow and develop, until, in the opinion of many, it was as advanced as that of any

American artist at the time. Despite this, she had not had a showing in several years, because she had been developing her oil-painting skills while Stieglitz was assembling his portrait of her in photographs. Eventually, she knew that the time had come for her work to be shown.

GOING PUBLIC

She started gradually. In April 1921, at the *Exhibition of Paintings and Drawings Showing the Later Tendencies in Art*, held at the Pennsylvania Academy of the Fine Arts, three of her paintings were shown, including *The Black Spot*. As usual, there was some resistance to having a woman artist in the exhibition, but since Stieglitz was the show's organizer, the academy had very little choice, as O'Keeffe recalled later:

> It was hard going as a woman. Arthur B. Carles of Philadelphia came in to Stieglitz and wanted him to hang a group show there. "But I don't want any [expletive deleted] women in the show," he told Stieglitz. "Take it or leave it," Stieglitz said. "There'll be no show without her."[3]

It was a start. O'Keeffe's life had begun to fall into a predictable pattern. Summers were spent in Lake George with Stieglitz's family. While Stieglitz enjoyed his traditional summer getaway, for O'Keeffe it was a time of too many people, too much family drama, and too little solitude. Converting a broken-down shanty located far from the main house into a studio helped, but O'Keeffe still found her time at Oaklawn confining.

What the summers did do, however, was allow her to recharge. Her imagination could go to work, providing her with the imagery that she would put down on her canvases during the fall and winter. By the summer of 1922, O'Keeffe

Georgia O'Keeffe's 1946 sculpture *Abstraction* exhibited at Gerard Peters Gallery in Santa Fe, New Mexico. Behind it, from left, are the O'Keeffe paintings *Only One*, 1959, and *From the Plains II*, 1954.

had begun to frame some of her paintings, putting as much attention into that as she did into preparing her canvases before painting. For O'Keeffe, her perfectionism extended from the first step of the artistic process right down to the very end.

She also began to realize the challenges she faced as a woman in what was then still a man's world. Stieglitz largely surrounded himself with male artists who happily argued about art theory and debated topics such as the French artist Paul Cézanne and the plastic quality of his form and color. O'Keeffe felt out of place in such discussions and had little interest in them anyway. "I was an outsider. My color and form were not acceptable. It had nothing to do with Cézanne or anyone else. I didn't understand what they were talking about."[4]

O'Keeffe's response to the men? Walking past her shanty art studio one day, she noticed how rundown it looked in the early morning light. She thought, "I can paint one of those dismal-colored paintings like the men. I think for fun I will try—all low-toned and dreary with the tree beside the door."[5]

That painting, along with 99 others, was on display at her first solo exhibition in six years, which opened at the Anderson Galleries on January 29, 1923. Interest in O'Keeffe had been growing ever since Stieglitz's photos had been shown two years earlier, while recent articles about her in *Vanity Fair*, the *New York Sun*, and *The Arts* served only to pique the curiosity of art lovers. The paintings were shown with only dates and numbers—no titles were given. The flyer for the show was equally unadorned:

Alfred Stieglitz
Presents
One Hundred Pictures
Oils, Water-colors
Pastels, Drawings
by
Georgia O'Keeffe
American

The show was an enormous success. More than 500 people came to see her show each day, intrigued that the subject of Stieglitz's photographic exhibition was a talented artist in her own right. They were drawn as well by reviews that discussed the undisguised feminine sexuality that emerged in her work. Critic Paul Rosenfeld wrote that "there is no stroke laid by her brush, whatever it is she may paint, that is not curiously, arrestingly, female in quality. Essence of very womanhood permeates her pictures."[6]

O'Keeffe reacted to the critics' sexual readings of her work with a mixture of embarrassment and anger. She had already decided, though, that the only critic of her art who truly mattered was herself: "I make up my own mind about it—how good or bad or indifferent it is. After that the critics can write what they please. I have already settled it for myself so flattery and criticism go down the same drain and I am quite free."[7]

The show ran for two weeks, and more than nine articles appeared, all in praise of her work. As an added bonus, 20 of her works sold for a total of $3,000. Much to O'Keeffe's amusement, *The Shanty*, her drab painting done purposely in a male painter's style, was one of those 20, purchased by art collector Duncan Phillips. "Among the artists at that time, it was disgraceful to think of anything pretty," O'Keeffe commented. "People felt that painting had to have a sort of dirty look. I felt I could make a dirty painting too, so I did. . . . The men seemed to approve of it."[8]

Winning the approval of men, however, was never part of her agenda. Joan Didion points out that, throughout her life, the words *the city men*, *the men*, and *they* crop up again and again in her writing. O'Keeffe knew that, as a woman artist, she would always be judged by men. But, with the possible exception of Alfred Stieglitz, what "the men" thought about her art was irrelevant. Indeed, her contempt for them only increased with their approval of *The Shanty*. Fifty-four years after that painting sold, she contemptuously commented: "They seemed to think that maybe I was beginning to paint. That was my only low-toned, dismal-colored painting."[9]

CHILDREN AND ART

While Stieglitz had moved in with O'Keeffe in 1918, it was not until 1922 that his divorce from his wife became final. Now that it was legally possible, Stieglitz began to pressure O'Keeffe to marry him. It took another two years to convince her, during which time O'Keeffe, now in her mid-30s, finally gave up on the idea of ever having a child with him. The woman whose art spoke to many viewers about her want of a child, concluded that Stieglitz, now in his 60s, had no interest in becoming a father again. Given that her options were to stay with Stieglitz and devote her life to art or leave him to become a mother, it comes as little surprise that she chose art.

She also gave in to Stieglitz's demand that she marry him. On December 11, 1924, Stieglitz and O'Keeffe took the ferry from New York City to New Jersey, where it was easier for a divorced man to marry. They exchanged traditional vows, with the notable exception of O'Keeffe not vowing to "love, honor, and obey." On the car ride back to the ferry, the driver, artist John Marin, had a minor car accident. Nobody was hurt, but, as Laurie Lisle described the scene, "Georgia remarked grimly that she felt as if she had lost a leg. The way the story was repeated, no one was ever quite sure whether she meant that the accident or her wedding felt like an amputation."[10]

Irrevocably committed to life as an artist, O'Keeffe continued to find new ways to expand her art. She began to explore the concept of "equivalents," an idea that she borrowed from Stieglitz. In 1921, Stieglitz began a series of photographs of the clouds over Lake George. In these photographs, he tried to create an artistic and emotional intensity similar to that of his relationship with O'Keeffe. Lisle, in her biography of O'Keeffe, notes that some photographs of low-lying clouds, lit from behind by the sun, seem to be "electrified by a powerful emotional charge."[11]

In other photos, Stieglitz seemed to find female forms in the rippling edges of the clouds.

O'Keeffe took his concept and applied it to a different subject. She had long considered the possibility of painting flowers but realized that she could not give the viewer the exact same experience of enjoyment that she acquired from them. Instead, she began to contemplate finding equivalents to recreate for the viewer the feeling that she had had. "I know I cannot paint a flower . . . but maybe in terms of paint color I can convey to you my experience of the flower or the experience that makes the flower of significance to me at that particular time."[12] With that, O'Keeffe slowly found her way to one of the subjects that most defined her artistic identity to the general public: flowers.

Through his photography, Stieglitz—and his followers—influenced her art in other ways as well. Lisle observed:

> Although Stieglitz didn't make blowups or use bizarre angles, younger cameramen around him did, and Georgia noticed. She was known to paint only a fragment of an object or to place it off-center like a cropped photo. The distortion of the lens seemed evident in other compositions in which forms were tilted or receded in unrealistic ways. Working alongside the young medium of photography gave O'Keeffe a fresh viewpoint and the license to break painterly rules.[13]

Some of these new paintings were displayed in O'Keeffe's next show, a dual exhibition with Stieglitz. His cloud photographs hung in one room, O'Keeffe's paintings in the other. The exhibit, which opened on February 28, 1924, was another huge step forward in O'Keeffe's career. Nearly absent was the abstract art of her previous exhibitions, and in its place was her new representative style of equivalents: pictures of trees, calla lilies, sunflowers, avocados, and trees predominated.

But if O'Keeffe thought that her move from abstraction to representational art would silence the discussion of sexual symbolism in her work, she was mistaken. "All Miss O'Keeffe's paintings are intimate, some of them almost unbearably so," wrote Vergil Barker in *The Arts*.[14] Indeed, critic Henry McBride felt that O'Keeffe's sexuality was more apparent in her calla lilies than in the tunnels of her more abstract works.

Her flowers began to grow larger and larger. What she wanted to do, she said, was force viewers to take the time to really look at a flower in a way they perhaps had never done before.

> A flower is relatively small. Everyone has many associations with a flower—the idea of flowers. [. . .] Still—in a way—nobody sees a flower—really—it is so small—we haven't time—and to see takes time, like to have a friend takes time. [. . .] So I said to myself—I'll paint what I see—what the flower is to me but I'll paint it big and they will be surprised into taking time to look at it—I will make even busy New Yorkers take time to see what I see of flowers.[15]

After she completed her first gigantic flower painting in 1924, she invited Stieglitz to be the first person to see it. Initially, he did not know what to think. "I don't know how you're going to get away with anything like that—you aren't planning to show it, are you?"[16] O'Keeffe, confident in her work, knew that the painting was good.

Other factors went into the development of her giant flowers as well. Writer Benita Eisler points out that they were in some ways a symbol of their era: It was a time when size (such as in the giant skyscrapers popping up all

O'Keeffe is perhaps best known for her large paintings of flowers. Seen here on display at an April 2007 exhibition in Shanghai, China, is *Red Poppy No. VI*.

over New York City) became a measure of fame and success. O'Keeffe acknowledged this: "I realized that were I to paint the same flowers so small, no one would look at them because I was unknown. So I thought I'll make them big like the huge buildings going up. People will be startled—they'll *have* to look at them—and they did."[17]

O'Keeffe was right—people did look at them. Her first showing of her new effort was in 1925: *Alfred Stieglitz Presents Seven Americans: 159 Paintings, Photographs & Things, Recent and Never Before Publicly Shown, by Arthur G. Dove, Marsden Hartley, John Marin, Charles Demuth, Paul Strand, Georgia O'Keeffe, Alfred Stieglitz.* Despite the competition, it was O'Keeffe's work that made the great impression. Writer and critic Edmund Wilson said in the *New Republic* that she had "outblazed the work of the men around her."[18]

As biographer Laurie Lisle describes the paintings, "Her gigantic flowers, which were painted frontally and revealingly, . . . had the effect of firmly diminishing the human beings who stood in front of them. . . . [A reviewer wrote,] 'It is as if we humans were butterflies.'"[19] Indeed, these paintings, seen as if from the perspective of an approaching butterfly or bee, can be easily compared to photographs of water lilies taken by Stieglitz a decade earlier.

Art critic Britta Benke points out that, in a typical O'Keeffe flower painting, such as *Two Calla Lilies on Pink* (1928), the entire canvas is filled by just one or two blooms:

> These are painted in extreme close-up, as a result of which the outer edges of the leaves and stems are often cut off. The larger picture must thus be completed in the viewer's mind. Through their magnification, the flowers are taken out of their natural context and acquire a special, outsized significance. The close-up angle permits a detailed examination of the individual structure of each bloom.[20]

With her giant flower paintings, O'Keeffe could not avoid the sexual interpretations of her earlier works. Biographer Laurie Lisle writes:

> Her trembling, feathery, unfurling petals reminded people of genitalia just as the abstractions had done . . . [S]tamens and corollas suggested male genitals, while dark recesses that invited penetration strongly suggested female vulvas. One woman who owned a big O'Keeffe flower painting was shocked to discover someone teaching a child the facts of life from it. When she hastily rehung it in her bedroom, a friend remarked, "Oh, I'm so glad you moved that vagina out of the living room."[21]

For her part, O'Keeffe denied any sexual implications in her art and felt strongly that such interpretations were only in eye of the beholder. She wrote in an exhibition catalog:

> Well—I made you take time to look at what I saw and when you took time to really notice my flower you hung all your associations with flowers on my flower and you write about my flower as if I think and see what you think and see of the flower—and I don't.[22]

By the end of the 1920s, O'Keeffe was not only famous, but she was widely considered to be the nation's greatest female artist. What angered her, not surprisingly, is that she felt she was being insulted by being labeled as a woman artist. "The men like to put me down as the best woman painter," she said in 1943. "I think I'm one of the best painters."[23]

MORE THAN JUST FLOWERS

One reason she was categorized as a female artist throughout the 1920s was that her primary subject matter during that period was flowers. Indeed, her name became so synonymous with flowers, and with the calla lily in particular, that when Mexican artist Miguel Covarrubias caricatured O'Keeffe for a 1929 issue of the *New Yorker*, she was shown as "Our Lady of the Lily: Georgia O'Keeffe." During this period, however, O'Keeffe worked on paintings with other subjects as well, including one that was primarily male in more ways than one: skyscrapers.

Throughout the 1920s, skyscrapers were being built all across New York City. O'Keeffe was fascinated by their development and often wondered what it would be like to live so high in the sky. Stieglitz, too, had become fascinated with skyscrapers and saw them as symbolizing the raw energy of the city. In 1925, the couple moved into an apartment on the top floor, the thirty-fifth, of the Shelton Hotel.

Over the next five years, O'Keeffe painted more than 20 urban landscapes, showing a New York City that is extremely personal, atmospheric, and romantic. "One can't paint New York as it is, but rather as it is felt," O'Keeffe once noted.[24] She began to paint the new city rising up around her. She did several paintings of the Shelton Hotel, including *The Shelton with Sunspots* (1926), in which O'Keeffe plays with the image of solarized disks against the strong lines of the hotel. She did paintings of views from their apartment window: scenes showing skies ranging from bright blue to dismal gray, the East River with its boats and barges looking like toys from her perspective, with the factories and smokestacks in the borough of Queens seen in the distance.

In other paintings, O'Keeffe emphasizes the more claustrophobic aspects of the city. Painted from street level looking up, the buildings appear to be converging, closing the viewer in. The buildings themselves are not the focal point of the paintings, and the details are left sketchy. The emphasis is on the play of the sky behind the buildings.

Georgia O'Keeffe in 1945. The role of the personal was central to her development as an artist.

Once again, as in her earlier abstracts, it is the blue *behind* the nominal topic that is the idea of the painting.

This series of urban paintings, moving from night scenes to day, from scenes looking down at the city below, from scenes looking up at the skyscrapers looming

THE ROLE OF THE PERSONAL

Like any great artist, O'Keeffe was able to find her subjects as they happened. After her 1927 operation to remove a lump from her breast, she created one of her most powerful and personal works. Named *Black Abstraction*, it was taken from the last conscious image she had before going into surgery:

> I was on a stretcher in a large room, two nurses hovering over me, a very large bright skylight above me. I had decided to be conscious as long as possible. I heard the doctor washing his hands. The skylight began to whirl and slowly become smaller and smaller in a black space. I lifted my right arm overhead and dropped it. As the skylight became a small white dot in a black room, I lifted my left arm over my head. As it started to drop and the white dot became very small, I was gone.*

The painting that emerged, a black halo surrounding a tiny speck of light, with the faint outline of an arm at the bottom of the picture, is a stunning representation of her experience, of *the* experience of going under anesthesia before surgery.

---

*Benita Eisler, *O'Keeffe & Stieglitz: An American Romance*. New York: Penguin Books, 1991, p. 363.

overhead, showed her love and fascination with the city. By using perspectives learned from photographs by Stieglitz, she presented the viewer with her own individual view of the city. Art critic Britta Benke proclaimed, "Georgia O'Keeffe's unique achievement in her paintings was to render visible the intangible charisma and fascination of New York City."[25]

By 1928, though, O'Keeffe's interest in New York was beginning to fade. In some ways, her career was at a peak: her shows were popular, her paintings were selling quite well (in 1928 an anonymous French collector purchased six of her calla lily paintings for the then-astronomical sum of $25,000—the equivalent of several hundred thousand dollars today), and her reputation as an artist was as high as it had ever been. Lewis Mumford, writing in 1927, said that, because O'Keeffe constantly created new forms, she was the most original painter in America. As an artist, things were going well.

On a personal level, though, things were different. Summers at Lake George, always difficult, had become nearly impossible. O'Keeffe, who needed privacy and time to think and paint, was constantly surrounded by members of Stieglitz's large family. This made her tense and unhappy, and strained her relationship with Stieglitz. Not only was she finding it impossible to create, she felt that she had "used up" Lake George—she had painted everything there that she wanted to paint.

She began to suffer health problems as well. In July 1927, she discovered a lump in her breast. The next month, a benign tumor was removed. At 39, it was O'Keeffe's first real brush with her own mortality. It scared her, forcing her to consider her priorities, and her need to create the time and space in order to work.

Despite the difficulties surrounding her, O'Keeffe went ahead with her annual art show in 1929. For the first time

MABEL DODGE LUHAN

Mabel Dodge Sterne Luhan (February 26, 1879–August 13, 1962) was a wealthy patron of the arts and the center of the art colony in Taos, New Mexico.

Born in Buffalo, New York, Luhan was the daughter of a wealthy banker. Her first marriage, to the son of a steamship owner, ended in tragedy when he died in a hunting accident. She then married Edwin Dodge, a wealthy architect, and lived in Florence, Italy, from 1905 to 1912. There, she entertained local artists as well as noted writers like Gertrude Stein and André Gide.

Returning to the United States, she settled in Greenwich Village in New York City, where she set herself up as patron of the arts, loaning money to needy artists and holding a weekly "salon" in her Fifth Avenue apartment. Luminaries like Emma Goldman, John Reed, "Big Bill" Haywood, and Carl Van Vechten were regulars at her house. After Dodge took Reed as a lover, she returned to France, where she socialized with Stein and Pablo Picasso.

After stints in New York and Provincetown, Massachusetts, Dodge and Reed broke up, and she took up with and married painter Maurice Sterne, with whom she went to Taos, New Mexico, in 1919. There, on the advice of Native American Tony Luhan, she bought a 12-acre property. Luhan set up a teepee in front of the couple's house, and drummed there every night until Mabel came to him. Mabel and Maurice soon divorced, and in 1923, she married Luhan, making him her fourth and final husband.

She remained in Taos the rest of her life, where she entertained, gave financial assistance to, and did everything she could to help deserving artists. After her death in 1962, her house was designated a national historic landmark and is now a historic inn and conference center.

in her career, it was not a success. There were very few new paintings to show. And while paintings like *Calla Lilies on Red* were described by critic Murdock Pemberton as being "as exciting a painting as anything we have seen this season," most critics saw the exhibit as weak, with work that showed an artist in a state of transition.[26]

O'Keeffe could not have agreed more. She wrote, "The encouraging note I want to add is that I hope not to have an exhibition again for a long—long—long time."[27] But if it was true that O'Keeffe was in a state of transition, nothing, including her art, would change as long as the situation of summers in Lake George continued.

For more than 10 years, O'Keeffe had repressed her own longings in favor of her husband's need for regular visits to Lake George and his family. Finally, though, she had had enough.

For some time, she had been hearing about a growing colony of artists in Taos, New Mexico. Then, in March 1929, her longtime friend Paul Strand had a new exhibit, showing photographs of his 1926 summer trip to northern New Mexico and Mesa Verde, Colorado. These photographs, illustrating the open landscapes of the American Southwest, reminded O'Keeffe of her years in Texas and her love of that kind of landscape.

That was all O'Keeffe needed. In April 1929, she left New York City without her husband, but accompanied by Paul Strand's wife, Beck, to spend the summer in Taos, New Mexico, armed with an invitation to stay with wealthy arts patron Mabel Dodge Luhan. The trip would prove fateful—it would profoundly affect her art and her life.

Finding Her True Home

"Like the dawn of the world."[1]

—Mabel Dodge Luhan,
describing the mystical qualities of Taos.

Georgia O'Keeffe and Beck Strand arrived in Santa Fe, New Mexico, where they were met by Mabel Dodge Luhan and her husband, Tony Luhan. They brought the pair to Luhan's Taos estate, where they were assigned the Pink House, a guest cottage that had recently been the home of English novelist D.H. Lawrence and his wife, Frieda.

O'Keeffe was instantly entranced by Taos. The light, the space, the openness, and the mountains—it was what she had always wanted. As biographer Laurie Lisle put it, "The place fitted her aesthetic temperament perfectly, and she was later to say that 'half your work is done for you' in New Mexico. . . . 'This is wonderful. No one told me that it was like *this!*'"[2]

In part, it was the bright New Mexican sunlight, which, combined with the high, clear altitude, gave visitors the impression that they were truly *seeing* for the first time. From the Taos highland, O'Keeffe could see for miles, watching the sky change, watching storm clouds build and disperse. The vastness of the spaces, especially in contrast to those in New York City and Lake George was exhilarating. "The world is wide here," she said about New Mexico, "and it's very hard to feel that it's wide in the East."[3]

Tony Luhan would take her on long drives throughout the area, visiting caves, waterfalls, mountains, and Indian pueblos. O'Keeffe was so happy on these trips that she asked Luhan to teach her how to drive. Although she got off to a rough start by smashing the car door against the side of the garage, she picked driving up quickly, even purchasing her own car, a Model A Ford, for $670.

DID YOU KNOW?

Santa Fe, New Mexico, is home to the Georgia O'Keeffe Museum. Opened in 1997, the museum has a collection of more than 3,000 works, including 1,149 drawings, watercolors, paintings, and sculptures done by O'Keeffe. Consisting of more than half of her life's work, it is the single largest collection of O'Keeffe's art held in one museum. The museum is also steward to both of O'Keeffe's New Mexico homes: her property at Ghost Ranch and her house in Abiquiú, both of which are open to public tours.

And, of course, Taos inspired her to paint. It gave her new landscapes, new architecture, new skies, and new colors to use. On her many walks through the desert landscape, she became interested in the large six-foot wooden crosses erected by a local Christian sect, which inspired several paintings, including *Black Cross with Stars and Blue*. She also did a series of paintings of the area's most famous church, Ranchos de Taos.

Ranchos de Taos had been the subject of many painters, but no one before O'Keeffe had ever painted it as she did, as an organic object that seemed to grow directly out of the hard New Mexican landscape. And instead of painting the church as a whole, she showed just a part of the wall, which stood out in bold relief against the blue southwestern sky.

When she left Taos in August to join Stieglitz in Lake George, she knew she would have to return. By February 1930, she was ready to show her new work. Two-thirds of her new paintings were inspired by her time in New Mexico. The subject matter was new for her, and once again, the critics were fascinated by yet another development in her art. Edward Alden Jewell, writing in the *New York Times*, proclaimed it the most exciting exhibition he had ever seen.

DEPRESSION, POLITICS, AFFAIRS

Others, however, were not so sure. The Great Depression, which had begun in October 1929, had thrown millions of people out of work. With so many people poor, so many people suffering, many artists began to think that their work should reflect the times and serve as a voice for the nation's poor and working classes. Against that kind of artistic theory, O'Keeffe's paintings of flowers and churches struck many as dated and out of place. For her part, O'Keeffe refused to change with the times. She believed that the purpose of art was to create beauty: politics and attempts to use art to educate the working class were, she felt, the wrong path for art.

In 1930, she again returned to Taos and the New Mexico landscapes she loved, leaving Stieglitz on his own at Lake George. O'Keeffe worked hard that summer, avoiding the company of Dodge Luhan and her entourage, and reveling in the pleasure of being alone in the desert. She did not need other people. New Mexico and her paints were all she required to be happy.

That summer, she also acquired a new fascination: the sun-baked animal bones found strewn throughout the desert. Although some found them ghoulish, for O'Keeffe, they were beautiful objects. In fact, she did not even think of them as bones. She looked at them in a completely different way, seeing them as "equivalents" of the desert, equivalents that would give her a way to explore the desert on canvas in a way that had never been done before. She explained her thinking in her 1939 exhibition catalog:

> I have wanted to paint the desert and I haven't known how. The bones seemed to cut sharply to the center of something that is keenly alive on the desert even tho' it is vast and empty and untouchable—and knows no kindness with all its beauty.[4]

There was one added bonus to her new fascination with bones. Unlike her paintings of flowers, it seemed unlikely that other artists would imitate her paintings of bones!

Once again, O'Keeffe returned in the fall to Lake George and Stieglitz. While she enjoyed and needed her time alone in Taos, a part of her felt guilty about abandoning her aging husband for the summer. "I feel I have two jobs," she told Dodge Luhan. "My own work—and helping him to function in his way."[5] Along with the rest of her belongings, she brought back with her a large barrel filled with sun-bleached animal bones. By the end of the year, Stieglitz was photographing O'Keeffe's long fingers exploring the eye socket and teeth of a horse's skull.

Despite their artistic relationship, the couple's *personal* relationship was becoming more strained. Stieglitz's refusal to travel to Taos, his declining career paralleling her ascendancy, his ever-growing hypochondria, and her increasing need for solitude all played their parts. Another woman was also on the scene, a young art student named Dorothy Norman.

Stieglitz began to photograph her, just as he had done with O'Keeffe years earlier. Lacking ambition for herself, Norman helped him in ways that O'Keeffe was unable to do. She did secretarial and bookkeeping work, and perhaps most important, worked tirelessly as fundraiser, bringing in enough money to enable Stieglitz to keep his latest gallery, An American Place, open. While O'Keeffe was understandably upset about the new woman in her husband's life, her career still came first. Once again, in the summer of 1931, she returned to New Mexico, where she found a way to use the skull and bones she had been collecting as a new basis for her art.

The first work was called *Horse's Skull with Pink Rose*, and it happened almost by accident. One evening, she had placed a horse's skull on her kitchen table. The next morning, she was walking past the skull holding a fake pink rose made of fabric, when "almost without thinking about what I was doing, I put the flower in the horse's eye and went to the door. On my return, I was so struck by the wonderful effect of the rose in the horse's eye that I knew that here was a painting that had to be done."[6] As was her usual pattern, other paintings followed, including *Horse's Skull with White Rose* and *Cow's Skull with White Calico Roses*. These paintings can appear gruesome at first sight. But, as art critic Hunter Drohojowska-Philp points out, "these animal death heads appear to be staring out of the canvas with a sort of jaunty gallows humor."[7]

O'Keeffe followed these three paintings with one that is considered one of her masterpieces, *Cow's Skull: Red, White, and Blue*. She said the work was her attempt to make a truly American painting that was, at the same time, deeply personal:

> As I was working I thought of the city men I had been seeing in the East. They talked so often of writing the Great American Novel—the Great American Play—the Great American Poetry. People wanted to "do" the American scene. I had gone back and forth across the country several times by then, and some of the current ideas about the American scene struck me as pretty ridiculous. To them, the American scene was a dilapidated house with a broken-down buckboard out front and a horse that looked like a skeleton. I knew America was very rich and lush. Well, I started painting my skulls around this time. . . . I had lived in the cattle country— Amarillo was the crossroads of cattle shipping, and you could see the cattle coming in across the range for days at a time. For goodness' sake, I thought, the people who talk about the American scene don't know anything about it. So, in a way, that cow's skull was my joke on the American scene, and it gave me pleasure to make it in red, white, and blue.[8]

When she displayed her new skull and flower paintings at her 1932 show, critics were stunned by the work, described as both occult and surrealistic. "What will she find to top this year's splendid salutation of the dead I cannot imagine," a reviewer for *Art News* remarked, "but it's a wide world and Miss O'Keeffe is not one to loiter along the way."[9]

Seen here, O'Keeffe poses with one of her most recognizable works, *Cow's Skull: Red, White, and Blue*, 1931.

BREAKDOWN

Aware of the growing competition from the younger Dorothy Norman, O'Keeffe did not to go New Mexico in the summer of 1932, opting instead to summer in Lake George with Stieglitz. Tensions between the couple were still high, and she found it difficult to get any work done. New Mexico, she increasingly felt, was where she needed to be for her art.

On top of her difficulties in painting, she was facing increased competition from other women artists, including her sisters Ida and Catherine, whose close-up paintings of flowers seemed to be taken entirely from their older sister's work. Feeling artistically challenged, O'Keeffe accepted an offer to paint a mural on the walls and ceiling of Radio City Music Hall's second-mezzanine powder room. The Depression had seen an explosion of publicly commissioned murals, but O'Keeffe was the first woman to receive such an offer, and she was eager to take up the challenge.

It turned out to be a mistake. Stieglitz was opposed to the idea, attacking the craze for murals as "that Mexican disease called murals."[10] He tried to kill the contract she had signed, but to no avail. O'Keeffe set to work, but it did not go well. The work took longer than she expected, and the size of the room itself, covering hundreds of square feet of surface, proved to be too much for her. Six weeks before the theater was due to open, when part of her work began to peel off the wall, she snapped, becoming furiously angry before bursting into tears.

She had reached the end of her rope. Unable to work, sleep, eat, or even walk, on February 1, 1933, O'Keeffe entered Doctors Hospital in Manhattan for treatment. She had had a nervous breakdown. O'Keeffe was in treatment for seven weeks. During that time, Stieglitz showed an exhibition of her work, old and new, at An American Place. The show received nearly unanimous praise, with Ralph Flint of *Art News* claiming that the look at her previous work showed that she had a talent "ripe with beauty, touched by grace, buoyant with vision, sure in execution, clear as to character."[11]

She spent the next year recovering, traveling to Bermuda, summering in Lake George, establishing a close relationship with the African-American writer Jean Toomer, and visiting New York City. What she was not doing was painting. It was her longest time away from a canvas since 1908. Her only showings during this period were retrospectives, which served to keep her before the public eye, and earned needed money when her works sold.

Finally, she had recovered sufficiently both mentally and physically to do what she needed to do. Her relationship with Stieglitz had evolved from being one of passion to one of companionship. Art was the center of her life, but she was unable to do anything while in New York. For her own sake and for the sake of her art, she needed to return to New Mexico.

Ghost Ranch

It had been almost three years since she was last in New Mexico. This time, however, she was a woman on a mission. For years, she had been hearing about the Ghost Ranch, an area many of her friends had described as the most beautiful place in the world. On previous trips to New Mexico, she had tried to find it, but could not. This time, however, the fates steered her in the right direction.

One afternoon, while shopping at a small local store, she saw a car parked outside with the initials "GR" on it. Finding the car's driver, she received somewhat mysterious directions to the legendary ranch: Follow the road from Española to a spot where there was an animal skull—if, of course, the skull was still there.

She set out the next day to find it. Driving 40 miles (64 kilometers) from where she was staying in Alcalde, she crossed wooden bridges and drove down dirt roads until she found the spot with the skull. She then turned right and crossed a low narrow bridge. Before long, she found it—a cluster of ranch buildings beneath a golden mesa. She would later recall that as the moment she knew it was the place where she was going to live.

Much to her dismay, though, upon arriving at Ghost Ranch she learned that the owner, Arthur Newton Pack, a wealthy conservationist and publisher of *Nature* magazine, had turned it into a dude ranch. Here, rich Easterners came to pretend to live like cowboys for a few weeks at a time. O'Keeffe was uncertain about what the place would be like, since, as she later said, "I thought dude ranchers were a lower form of life."[1] Still, attracted by the beauty of the surroundings, when she learned that a room was available for one night in the oldest ranch building, Ghost House, she leapt at the opportunity.

Her night at the ranch only confirmed her strong feelings about the place, and then, to her good fortune, she learned that a family had been forced to leave the ranch due to illness, freeing space for her. She packed up her belongings at the H and M Ranch, where she had been staying, and quickly returned to Ghost Ranch, where she spent the remainder of the summer.

She hiked miles every day. She drove everywhere she could in the area, exploring canyons and cliffs, always on the lookout for new landscapes, new vistas, and new scenes to paint. She had already rigged her Model A Ford to be a mobile studio. She had removed the front passenger seat, and by loosening the bolts on the driver's seat, she could swivel around to paint with her canvas propped up against the back seat. The car's high roof gave her enough room to squeeze in her largest canvases: 30 by 40 inches (76 by 102 centimeters).

Inspired by new landscapes, mountains, mesas, and colors, O'Keeffe produced an extraordinarily high number of paintings that summer. She painted traditional Native American kachina dolls and a turkey feather next to a rusty horseshoe. She painted her trademark flowers, including her masterpiece *Blue Morning Glories*. She painted the rugged landscapes surrounding Ghost Ranch in paintings such as *Purple Hills No. II.*

She also created what some think of as her key painting of the year, *Ram's Head, White Hollyhock–Hills*. Against a gray-clouded sky, above a series of red hills speckled with green scrub, a ram's skull with a particularly full set of horns floats, somewhat mysteriously, next to a single white hollyhock blossom. "I had looked out on the hills for weeks and painted them again and again," she later recalled. "I don't remember where I picked up the head—or the hollyhock. Flowers were planted among the vegetables in the garden between the house and the hills and I probably picked up the hollyhock one day as I walked past. My paintings sometimes grow by pieces from what is around."[2] As is the case with many artists, the idea behind their inspiration is often mysterious, even to the artists themselves.

When *Ram's Head, White Hollyhock–Hills* was shown in her 1936 New York exhibition, it received the lion's share of attention. Lewis Mumford, writing in the January 18 issue of the *New Yorker*, noted:

> The epitome of the whole show is the painting of the ram's head, with its horns acting like wings, lifted up against the gray, wind-swept clouds; at its side is a white hollyhock flower. In conception and execution this is one of the most brilliant paintings O'Keeffe has done. Not only is it a piece of

O'Keeffe (*top row, third from left*) is photographed on March 22, 1935 at a dinner given for career women at the Hotel Astoria in New York City. During this period, she was at the height of her creative powers.

consummate craftsmanship, but it likewise possesses that mysterious force, that hold upon the hidden soul, which distinguishes important communication from the casual reports of the eye.[3]

Indeed, throughout the late 1930s, O'Keeffe was perhaps near the peak of her artistic creativity. In her next show, in 1937, 20 new paintings were shown. Among them was one of her most famous paintings, *Summer Days*. This painting shows an enormous deer's skull, its antlers extended to the upper edges of the painting, floating over a mountainous desert landscape. The skull is shown straight on, staring directly at the viewer. Wildflowers are shown beneath it, and beyond the mountains, a storm is gathering. As critic Britta Benke points out, "The artist is . . . interested in the objective beauty of her subjects. . . . Although realistically portrayed, the objects hover between space and time."[4] That painting, and the accompanying exhibition, earned O'Keeffe a featured article in *Time* magazine, a rare achievement for any artist, male or female.

The next year saw the creation of yet another O'Keeffe masterpiece: *From the Faraway, Nearby*. In this painting, the flowers are gone; all that remains, in the words of Laurie Lisle, is:

> An immense pair of elk's antlers soaring suspended in an ethereal pinkish-blue dawn over snow-capped mountains viewed with an extraordinary clarity. Like the other pictures of skulls in the sky, this one also seemed to have been painted from an elevated vantage point, as if the artist herself were levitating on a shimmering desert heat wave.[5]

SETTLING IN

Although much of her time was spent in and around New York City with Stieglitz, New Mexico seemed more and more to be her true home. At Ghost Ranch, she had moved out of the guesthouses and into her own private house, a building that Pack had built three miles (five kilometers) away from the ranch, named Rancho de los Burros.

The building was a small U-shaped adobe house, with whitewashed rooms built around a patio, and bedroom windows with a dramatic view of nearby cliffs. "As soon as I saw it, I knew I must have it," she said later. "I can't understand people who want something badly but don't grab for it. I grabbed."[6] Three years later, in 1940, she purchased Rancho de los Burros from the Packs. It was the first house she had ever owned.

Rancho de los Burros gave her everything she had wanted—the privacy she craved and the chance to live in a simple, yet beautiful house. Best of all, it gave her the landscapes she required as part of her life. The house's location had been selected for its superb view of the Pedernal, a flat-topped mesa in the Jemez range, about 10 miles (16 kilometers) to the southeast. O'Keeffe often described it as "a perfect blue mountain," and began to make it a part of her artistic landscape.[7]

"It's my private mountain," she often joked. "It belongs to me. God told me if I painted it enough, I could have it."[8] In her house, there was a ladder that allowed O'Keeffe to climb up to the roof, where she would sit for hours, watching the colors on the cliffs shift and fade with the everchanging light. "A pretty good backyard!" she would boast to guests.[9]

A REPUTATION AT ITS PEAK

At this point in her career, O'Keeffe was a star of the art world. Her work was displayed in shows worldwide and received great acclaim. Curiously enough, her looks began to get nearly as much attention in the media as her paintings. True, her first touch of fame had been through Stieglitz's photographs of her, but now she was becoming known for her own strikingly individual looks. As her fame spread, she began to appear in magazines with a vast readership, including a photographic essay in *Life* magazine in 1938.

But with increased attention came increased criticism. Her 1938 show drew sharp attacks. Critics accused O'Keeffe of spending too much time painting flowers and skulls. O'Keeffe was indifferent to the criticism: She was painting for herself, she felt, not for the critics.

Despite some negative reviews, her work began to be seen as a whole and recognized for its extraordinary artistic value. She was given an honorary doctorate of fine arts from the College of William and Mary in Williamsburg, Virginia. For O'Keeffe, whose only degree was a high school diploma, it was an honor she was proud to receive.

She also began a round of traveling: New York to New Mexico, New Mexico to California, California to Hawaii. By the time she returned to New York City in May 1939, she was near exhaustion and close to having a relapse of her breakdown of six years earlier. On doctor's orders not to travel, she spent the rest of that spring and summer in New York City, recovering slowly.

While still under a doctor's care, she was named, along with other notables such as Eleanor Roosevelt and Helen Keller, as one of the 12 most outstanding women of the last 50 years by a committee of the New York World's Fair. By the fall, she had recovered from her exhaustion and was ready to begin to paint again. She was also now, as Laurie Lisle pointed out, "the most famous, most successful woman painter in America."[10]

DID YOU KNOW?

In 1939, Georgia O'Keeffe was brought to Hawaii by the Dole Pineapple Company to do a painting of pineapples that could be used in an advertising campaign. She struggled with the commission, first presenting the company with a painting of a papaya, a fruit sold by Dole's competitors, before finally completing a painting that could be used to convince the American public that pineapple juice was good for them.

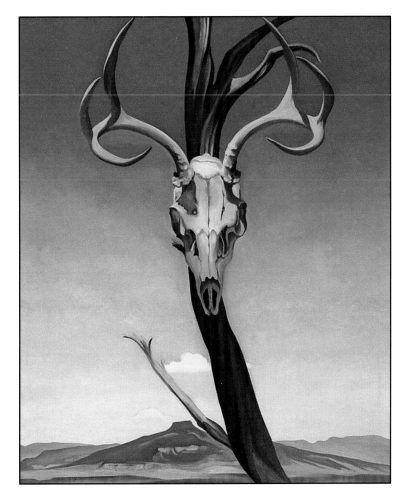

O'Keeffe's *Deer's Skull with Pedernal*, 1936, on display at the Museum of Fine Arts in Boston, Massachusetts. In the late 1930s, art critics who felt she was painting "too many flowers and skulls" often attacked her work.

Because she was the best-known woman painter in America, museums began to show retrospectives of her work, allowing audiences to see the entire range of her art, from her earliest abstract work through her flowers and all the way to her skulls and New Mexican landscapes. The first of these retrospectives was held at the Art Institute of Chicago in 1943.

It must have been an extraordinary experience for O'Keeffe. In 1905, she had attended the Art Institute as a student, uncertain where her art would take her. Now, on January 31, 1943, 61 of her most important works were on display. Museum curator Daniel Catton Rich wrote in the catalog that accompanied the retrospective:

> Seen in the whole her art betrays a perfect consistency. It has undergone no marked changes of style but has moved outward from its center. In over a quarter of a century of painting, O'Keeffe has only grown more herself.[11]

Three years later, the Museum of Modern Art in New York City presented its own retrospective of her work—the first time the museum had so honored a woman artist.

That June, as usual, O'Keeffe left for New Mexico, leaving Stieglitz, elderly and frail, in the care of a housekeeper. One month later, he suffered a cerebral thrombosis, a type of stroke, and O'Keeffe quickly flew back to New York to be by his side. He died on July 13, 1946, at age 82. O'Keeffe, his companion of almost 40 years, took his ashes to his beloved Lake George and buried them at the foot of a tall pine tree beside the lake.

Although their relationship had grown distant over the years, he remained an important presence in her life. He was her mentor, her business adviser, her husband. To recover from the painful loss, O'Keeffe returned to New Mexico, where she spent the summer and fall walking through the desert landscape, recalling her life with Stieglitz. She also painted a picture with red hills and sky that included a hidden personal tribute to her late husband. The painting, *A Black Bird with Snow-Covered Red Hills* depicts a stylized crow, a tribute to Stieglitz's nickname: "Old Crow Feather."

Without Stieglitz, she now had the solitary life she had always longed for. She was now a woman alone.

A Woman
on Her Own

Despite the difficulties and infidelities in Georgia
O'Keeffe's relationship with Alfred Stieglitz, it still
took her several years to come to terms with her loss. She
had to forgive him for his relationship with Dorothy Norman. She had to resolve her own feelings of guilt for abandoning him so often for her art. And, finally, as executor
of his will, she had to decide the best way to distribute his
collection of 850 works of art, thousands of photographs,
and more than 50,000 letters to various institutions. (She
inherited from Stieglitz a sizable estate of $148,000 in cash
and stocks.)

There was also a retrospective of Stieglitz's work to
assemble, and work to be done on her second home in
New Mexico. While she loved her house at Ghost Ranch,

water for gardening was unavailable, and O'Keeffe tired of having to drive many miles to purchase canned food and wilted vegetables. For years, she had had her eye on an abandoned hacienda in nearby Abiquiú, a tiny village that was home to Native Americans and descendents of

HER GARDEN AND DIET

Once her house at Abiquiú was restored, Georgia O'Keeffe set to work creating a garden that would allow her to grow the food she needed. She would get up at dawn to work before the New Mexico sun got high, first planting ordinary vegetables, before branching out into more exotic ones. Fig, mulberry, and almond trees were planted to provide shade for the young plants. And, being a woman ahead of her time, the garden was wholly organic. For example, when grasshoppers invaded it, instead of using insecticides, she brought turkeys into the garden to eat the insects.

Always interested in good food and healthy eating, she learned how to dry, pickle, freeze, and store her harvests, allowing her to eat well throughout the year. Known as a good cook, she often read cookbooks at night before falling asleep. While she enjoyed eating "gourmet" food, her diet most of the time was simple and basic: a cup of tea in the morning, followed by a big breakfast (probably a lifetime habit from her childhood on a farm), a cup of yogurt for a midday snack, a lunch of a soufflé and salad, followed by a light supper of fruits, vegetables, and cheeses. By maintaining a healthy diet and active lifestyle, O'Keeffe managed to keep her weight at a fit 127 pounds (58 kilograms) for most of her life.

Spanish settlers. There was water available for her own vegetable garden, along with a dilapidated house with a collapsed roof, handmade wooden doors, crumbling adobe walls, and a door in a long patio that struck her as interesting for reasons she did not quite understand. After the house became hers in 1945, repairs began to make it livable once again. She was the first white person to own a home in the village in its 200-year history.

For all these reasons, O'Keeffe did very little work during this period, but by 1948, she was slowly starting to paint again, beginning with a large gentle canvas, *Spring*. The following year, she was elected, along with other luminaries such as novelist Christopher Isherwood and poet E.E. Cummings to the National Institute of Arts and Letters. She was one of a very small number of women to have received the honor.

MAKING NEW MEXICO HOME

By 1949, it was time to put New York City behind her, a place where she had lived, at least part time, for more than 30 years. After painting for the first time a picture of the Brooklyn Bridge at the age of 61, she moved permanently to New Mexico, arriving in Abiquiú in time for spring.

Throughout the 1950s, O'Keeffe kept a relatively low profile, far from the public eye. Her life began to fall into a pattern: fall, winter, and early spring were spent in Abiquiú; the remainder of the year at Ghost Ranch. Of course, she painted, and her style began to change and to simplify as her own life became simpler. Her most important paintings of this period studied the architecture of the area, in particular her adobe home in Abiquiú. This series, as Benita Eisler describes it, started out predictably with a relatively realistic painting of her patio space, complete with ladder. The paintings that followed became progressively simpler: the black patio door is a constant; what

Pictured, Galley 8 of the Georgia O'Keeffe Museum in Santa Fe, New Mexico. At center is *Spring*, 1948. The other paintings on display are, from left to right, *Black Rock on Red*, 1971; *Black Hollyhock Blue Larkspur*, 1930; *Pelvis Series, Red with Yellow*, 1945; *Pelvis IV*, 1944; *Abstraction White Rose*, 1927; and *Patio Door with Green Leaf*, 1956.

changes is the play of color and the relationships between the rectangular figures.

These pictures appear almost childlike in their simplicity, but they are much more than that. With their careful play of color and shape, they harken back to her years in teaching the Dow method, when she asked her students to begin by putting a door in a square to get them to think about dividing space. And, as Eisler notes, the paintings give full display to O'Keeffe's own sophisticated views about how to divide space and use colors to establish a rhythm within the painting.

Although the patio series, as well as other paintings such as *Ladder to the Moon*, rank among her most interesting and captivating work, her reputation was on the decline. New trends in art, such as abstract expressionism, were growing in influence, and her work, if noted at all, was seen as a throwback to an earlier time, something of historic interest only.

O'KEEFFE IN ABIQUIÚ

When Georgia O'Keeffe first arrived in Abiquiú, her neighbors were a little scared of her. She was a woman living alone, who dressed in black and walked everywhere carrying a big walking stick, who collected rocks and skulls and bones—some townspeople, who had never had a white woman living in their midst, thought she was a witch.

As the years passed, O'Keeffe never quite managed to fit in. She refused to speak Spanish, and unlike nearly everyone else in town, did not attend the local Catholic church. Still, O'Keeffe and her neighbors, who were never able to understand either her or her art, reached enough of an understanding that allowed them to live together peacefully. And O'Keeffe did what she could to be a good neighbor.

When, for example, she learned that the well on her land was the only source of drinkable water in town, she used her own money to provide the village with a system that pumped water in from the mountains. She provided the money to purchase equipment that allowed the local television station to pick up educational programs. She helped to outfit the local boys with Little League uniforms and equipment, and sent them to games in outlying areas in her own car. And finally, when she heard some local boys complaining that there was no gymnasium to use, she provided the funding for a recreational center.

A piece of O'Keeffe's art on display at the Milwaukee Art Museum in May 2001. Hanging on the wall at right is her painting *Black Door with Snow*, 1955. As that painting demonstrates, O'Keeffe's art took on an almost child-like simplicity in her later life.

O'Keeffe, who had always painted largely to please herself, was indifferent to the new critical reaction to her work. She loved living in New Mexico year-round, and discovered, to her great surprise, that in some ways, winters were even better than summers. She loved the severe cold. She loved the way the piñon wood crackled in the fireplace. She loved the way the white snow looked piled on the roof of her adobe home.

O'Keeffe became ever more solitary, even going as far as to hire a deaf housekeeper so she did not need to talk. Her life revolved around exploring the New Mexican landscape and her art. She always had six blank canvases at the ready, "the hopefuls," she called them, for when inspiration struck her. After having painted for nearly half a century, she knew that the creative impulse could not be rushed—that when the time to paint came to her, she would know it. "I know what I'm going to do before I begin, and if there's nothing in my head, I do nothing," she often stated.[1]

EXPLORING THE WORLD

Of course, even Georgia O'Keeffe could not spend all of her time in solitary communion with her art and the New Mexican landscape. She took two Chinese chow puppies into her home and was quickly pleased with their companionship and their assistance in guarding her privacy. "They bite very well," she said once. "I've seen more than one pair of shoes filled with blood."[2]

Indeed, as O'Keeffe grew accustomed to her solitary life in New Mexico, she seemed to become more dismissive of the world around her. She complained bitterly about the constant intrusion into what she saw as "her" privacy, as cars and buses full of tourists came to see the famous artist at work. For many years, she would not even allow a telephone in her home, content to drive miles to the closest store to use its phone.

Yet, at the same time, for the first time in her life, she began to travel the world with friends. In 1951, she went to Mexico, where she had the opportunity to meet that

O'Keeffe photographed in Albuquerque, New Mexico, in 1960, as she adjusts her painting *Pelvis Series, Red with Yellow*, 1945.

country's most famous female artist, Frida Kahlo. In 1953, at the age of 65, she went to Europe for the first time and took in its artistic treasures. She went to the Louvre in Paris, was astonished by the cathedral at Chartres, and found herself surprised to enjoy the works of El Greco, Velázquez, and Goya, at the Prado museum in Madrid.

Also, somewhat surprisingly, while in France she turned down the opportunity to meet Pablo Picasso, the man many feel was the greatest artist of the twentieth century. Her reason? "I didn't care very much about looking at him, and

I'm sure he didn't care about looking at me. I don't speak French, so we couldn't talk," she explained later. "My companion thought it was heretical, but if you can't talk, what's the point?"[3]

For the next few years, her travels continued. Back for a summer in Spain. A trip to Peru. A three-month trip around the world in 1959 that included stops in Asia, where she was able to explore the world of Japanese painting that had always intrigued her, as well as a stop in Rome, where she expressed her intense dislike of the art at the Vatican. "The cherubs on the walls of the Vatican, dreadful. Those big naked things. Bigger than a man. Everything in Rome was like that to me—extraordinarily vulgar."[4]

No matter where she traveled, she was always happy to return home. When asked why she traveled so much, she often replied that it was to see for herself if she lived in the right place, and the answer was always "yes." O'Keeffe had so disappeared from the public's view that, in 1957, *Newsweek* magazine featured her in its "Where Are They Now?" column. That was about to change.

RETURNING TO HER PROPER PLACE

In 1960, the first major retrospective of her work since Stieglitz's death was held at the Worcester Art Museum in Massachusetts. More than a third of the paintings shown had been painted since 1946, including the patio series, new flower paintings, and a new series of paintings inspired by her flights around the world.

These pictures, done from the perspective of a bird looking down at the Earth, featured bold colors, showed river streams flowing through flattened landscapes, and were given such simple titles as *It Was Yellow and Pink* and *It Was Blue and Green*. These new paintings, which were presented alongside her earlier works, reminded critics why she mattered as an artist. Despite her age, she could still surprise them with her visions.

It was the beginning of a new reappraisal of her art and her life. Magazines took note of the exhibition. *Newsweek*, just years after the "Where Are They Now?" article, proclaimed her "the grand old lady of painting."[5] Not only was her art praised, but she herself was held up as an example of beauty 40 years after Stieglitz's photographs had made such an impression; *Look* magazine lauded her as an example of ageless beauty. As Laurie Lisle points out, "Her lines and wrinkles—on the expressive face of someone who had an intimate knowledge of solitude and endurance—appeared deliberate and even beautiful."[6]

But as always with Georgia O'Keeffe, there was new art to create. As we know, she had always been fascinated by the sky, and explored it through her art in many ways. "I suppose I could live in a jail as long as I had a little patch of blue sky to look at," she said in 1968.[7] Even her most ardent admirers, however, were surprised at her next series of paintings, which included the largest painting she had ever done.

Like her paintings of rivers done as seen from an airplane, her cloud paintings are also seen from above. "One day when I was flying back to New Mexico, the sky below was a most beautiful solid white. It looked so secure that I thought I could walk right out on it to the horizon if the door opened."[8] There were four paintings in the series, including *Sky Above Clouds IV* (1965), which measures 24 feet by 8 feet (7.3 meters by 2.4 meters), and holds a place of honor at the Art Institute of Chicago. It is this painting that inspired Quintana Didion's desire to meet the artist. It was the last major series of paintings that O'Keeffe completed.

LAST YEARS

Her final years were a time of honors and tragedy. In 1962, she was elected to the American Academy of Arts and

Letters, perhaps the nation's most prestigious honor society for the arts. Her art began to be shown more and more often, culminating in 1970 in a career-spanning exhibition

O'KEEFFE AND THE OVAL STONE

Along with collecting skulls and bones, Georgia O'Keeffe had always had a fascination with rocks. In 1961, while on a river-rafting trip on the Colorado River, she and fellow traveler, photographer Eliot Porter, had a good-natured competition to see who could collect the best and most highly polished river rocks. One evening, Porter found a rock, flat, smooth and black, that seemed to all concerned to be the perfect rock. Porter wanted to give it to his wife; O'Keeffe wanted it for herself.

Months later, O'Keeffe was at the Porters' home for Thanksgiving. The rock was proudly on display. When she thought that nobody was looking, O'Keeffe pocketed the rock for herself. In one telling of the story, she then quickly put the rock back, and the Porters graciously decided to give it to her. But, according to another version, she snuck the rock home, and eventually the Porters, not wanting to make a scene or lose a friendship, decided to just let her keep it. She kept the rock for the rest of her life, displayed on a shelf above her bed. Apparently, she had not changed a bit in the years since Alfred Stieglitz said about her, "When she wants something, she makes other people give it to her. They feel she is fine and has something other people do not."*

---

*Laurie Lisle, *Portrait of an Artist: A Biography of Georgia O'Keeffe*, New York: Washington Square Press, 1981, p. 387.

of 121 of her drawings and paintings at the Whitney Museum of American Art in New York.

This exhibition firmly established her as an icon in American art, one whose influence was felt throughout contemporary American art. She was awarded the Medal of Freedom, the nation's highest honor, in 1977. Around the same time, she found that she was an idol for the new generation of feminists, and became a representative of the modern, independent woman who lived life on her own terms.

For the most part, O'Keeffe rejected the newfound attention. She hated it when people showed up unannounced at her house to see a living legend for themselves. She still preferred her isolation in the stark simplicity of her New Mexico homes, surrounded by the landscapes she loved. However, she was getting older, and beginning in 1971, at the age of 84, she found it more and more difficult to live on her own.

She also discovered that her eyesight was fading. She lost her central vision, keeping only some peripheral sight. For an artist whose life revolved around her ability to see, it was a staggering loss. She began to live in a world composed only of simple patterns and shadows, and just doing the basic tasks of living became more and more difficult. It seemed likely that she would no longer be able to live the life she wanted.

In 1972, however, a young potter named Juan Hamilton knocked on her door, asking if she had any odd jobs that he could do for her. A strong relationship between the two quickly developed, and he became her closest confidant, companion, and business manager.

Hamilton provided O'Keeffe with the everyday assistance she needed, while encouraging her to continue painting. She began to paint again, working with an assistant to capture on canvas the colors and forms she could still see with her peripheral vision. These last paintings, done when she was nearly blind, appear to many to be a return to the kind of abstractions that first brought her to the attention of Alfred Stieglitz, when she was first finding herself as an artist. She also began to work in pottery and had a large kiln installed at the ranch for firing pots. Making art, despite her obvious handicaps, was still the most important part of her life.

By 1984, she was no longer able to live at either Ghost Ranch or her home in Abiquiú, and she moved to Santa Fe, where she lived with Hamilton and his family. Two years later, on March 6, 1986, Georgia O'Keeffe died at the age of 98. At her request, she was cremated, and her ashes were scattered over her beloved Ghost Ranch, the place where she could see the sky and hear the wind.

It seems a fitting end to a great American artist, one whose work constantly spoke to the power and endurance of nature. Through her art, she created images that will endure forever. And through her life, she demonstrated the importance of living as one wants and the necessity of creating one's own vision. O'Keeffe put to rest forever the notion that women are incapable of creating art that is as powerful and important as that done by any man. Her art and life will live on as shining examples of what is possible for generations to come.

CHRONOLOGY

1887   Georgia O'Keeffe is born on November 15 near Sun Prairie, Wisconsin.

1903   Georgia follows her family, who had moved a year earlier, to Williamsburg, Virginia.

1905   After graduating from Chatham Episcopal Institute, O'Keeffe enrolls at the Art Institute of Chicago; she is there for one year.

1907   After recovering at home from typhoid fever, O'Keeffe goes to New York City to study at the Art Students League.

1908   Family finances and a personal sense of uncertainty compel O'Keeffe to discontinue her education and move to Chicago to work as a commercial artist.

1912   O'Keeffe's interest in art is reborn after attending a summer class at the University of Virginia run by Alon Bement, a pupil of Arthur Wesley Dow's; she becomes a teaching assistant at the summer school, a position she holds until 1916. To gain further experience as a teacher, she works for two years in Amarillo, Texas.

1914   O'Keeffe enrolls at the Columbia University Teachers College in New York City.

1915   O'Keeffe takes a teaching position at Columbia College in South Carolina.

1916   Having achieved a personal breakthrough in her art, O'Keeffe sends her charcoal drawings known as *Specials* to her friend Anita Pollitzer, who shows them to renowned photographer Alfred Stieglitz; Stieglitz exhibits them at his New York gallery, 291; that fall, O'Keeffe accepts a position as head of the art department at the West Texas State Normal College in Canyon, where she remains through 1918.

1917   Stieglitz presents O'Keeffe's first solo show at 291; he also takes the first of the more than 500 photos of O'Keeffe that he will take over the course of his life.

1918   O'Keeffe moves to New York City, where Stieglitz is able to provide her with the financial and emotional support necessary for her to dedicate her life to her art; the two become lovers, even though Stieglitz is married.

1923   Stieglitz arranges the first large show of O'Keeffe's work, displaying more than 100 paintings at the Anderson Galleries.

1924   O'Keeffe and Stieglitz marry on December 11.

1925   In the *Seven Americans* show, the first of O'Keeffe's giant flower paintings are exhibited.

1927   O'Keeffe has two operations on her breasts; she refocuses her energies on herself and her art.

1929   At the invitation of Mabel Dodge Luhan, O'Keeffe travels to New Mexico for the first time. Enthralled by the land, she will regularly spend most of her summers there for the next 15 years, rarely traveling with Stieglitz to his summer home in Lake George, New York.

1930   The first exhibition of O'Keeffe's paintings of the American Southwest is presented at An American Place, Stieglitz's new gallery. She will present annual shows there through 1950.

1933   Suffering from a nervous breakdown, O'Keeffe is hospitalized for two months.

1934   O'Keeffe spends her first summer at Ghost Ranch in New Mexico, where, in 1940, she purchases a house and land.

1943   The Art Institute of Chicago holds the first major retrospective of her work.

1945   O'Keeffe purchases a second home in New Mexico, a rundown adobe structure in the village of Abiquiú; she will spend the next three years renovating her new home.

1946   The Museum of Modern Art in New York City stages a major retrospective of her work, the first time a female artist is so honored; on July 13, Alfred Stieglitz dies at the age of 82.

1949   O'Keeffe moves permanently to New Mexico, splitting her time between her houses at Ghost Ranch and Abiquiú.

1953   O'Keeffe makes her first trip to Europe, visiting France and Spain.

1959 O'Keeffe embarks on a three-month world tour.

1962 O'Keeffe is elected to the prestigious American Academy of Arts and Letters.

1970 O'Keeffe's largest career retrospective to date is held at the Whitney Museum of American Art in New York; the show reestablishes her reputation as a major American artist as well as introduces her work to a new generation of art lovers.

1971 O'Keeffe's eyesight begins to fail.

1972 Potter Juan Hamilton shows up at O'Keeffe's back door, asking for work; he soon establishes himself as her personal assistant and closest companion; Hamilton encourages her to continue to paint, as well as to begin to work with clay.

1986 Georgia O'Keeffe dies in Santa Fe, New Mexico, on March 6 at the age of 98.

NOTES

CHAPTER 1: FRUSTRATION

1. Laurie Lisle, *Portrait of an Artist: A Biography of Georgia O'Keeffe*. New York: Washington Square Press, 1981, p. 52.
2. Ibid., p. 53.
3. Ibid., p. 55.
4. Joan Didion, *We Tell Ourselves Stories in Order to Live: Collected Nonfiction*. New York: Everyman's Library, 2006, p. 271.
5. Ibid.
6. Ibid.
7. Britta Benke, *Georgia O'Keeffe 1887–1986: Flowers in the Desert*. New York: Barnes & Noble Books, 2001, p. 90.
8. Ibid., p. 88.

CHAPTER 2: THE EARLY YEARS

1. Lisle, *Portrait of an Artist*, p. 7.
2. Benita Eisler, *O'Keeffe & Stieglitz: An American Romance*. New York: Penguin Books, 1991, p. 13.
3. Lisle, *Portrait of an Artist*, p. 2.
4. Eisler, *O'Keeffe & Stieglitz*, p. 13.
5. Ibid.
6. Ibid., p. 15.
7. Lisle, *Portrait of an Artist*, p. 11.
8. Ibid.
9. Hunter Drohojowska-Philp, *Full Bloom: The Art and Life of Georgia O'Keeffe*. New York: W.W. Norton & Company, 2004, p. 19.
10. Lisle, *Portrait of an Artist*, p. 18.
11. Ibid., p. 19.
12. Ibid.
13. Drohojowska-Philp, *Full Bloom*, p. 28.
14. Lisle, *Portrait of an Artist*, p. 24.

15. Ibid., p. 27.
16. Ibid., p. 28.
17. Ibid., p. 29.
18. Eisler, *O'Keeffe & Stieglitz*, p. 20.
19. Ibid., p. 21.
20. Ibid.
21. Lisle, *Portrait of an Artist*, pp. 32–33.
22. Eisler, *O'Keeffe & Stieglitz*, p. 22.
23. Lisle, *Portrait of an Artist*, p. 35.
24. Eisler, *O'Keeffe & Stieglitz*, p. 22.
25. Ibid.

CHAPTER 3: STUDENT AND TEACHER

1. Lisle, *Portrait of an Artist*, p. 43.
2. Eisler, *O'Keeffe & Stieglitz*, p. 26.
3. Drohojowska-Philp, *Full Bloom*, p. 48.
4. Eisler, *O'Keeffe & Stieglitz*, p. 27.
5. Ibid.
6. Ibid.
7. Ibid., p. 28.
8. Ibid.
9. Ibid.
10. Lisle, *Portrait of an Artist*, pp. 59–60.
11. Eisler, *O'Keeffe & Stieglitz*, p. 59.
12. Lisle, *Portrait of an Artist*, p. 60.
13. Drohojowska-Philp, *Full Bloom*, p. 79.
14. Lisle, *Portrait of an Artist*, p. 63.
15. Eisler, *O'Keeffe & Stieglitz*, p. 62.
16. Lisle, *Portrait of an Artist*, p. 64.
17. Ibid.
18. Ibid., p. 70.
19. Ibid.
20. Ibid., p. 71.
21. Ibid., pp. 72–73.

22. Ibid., p. 74.
23. Ibid.
24. Ibid., p. 80.
25. Ibid., p. 81.
26. Ibid.
27. Ibid.

CHAPTER 4: FINDING A MENTOR, LOVER, AND FAME

1. Ibid. p. 82.
2. Drohojowska-Philp, *Full Bloom*, p. 103.
3. Lisle, *Portrait of an Artist*, p. 83.
4. Ibid.
5. Anita Pollitzer, *A Woman on Paper: Georgia O'Keeffe*. New York: Touchstone, 1988, pp. 43–46.
6. Drohojowska-Philp, *Full Bloom*, p. 106.
7. Ibid.
8. Ibid., p. 107.
9. Ibid.
10. Ibid.
11. Lisle, *Portrait of an Artist*, p. 92.
12. Ibid.
13. Drohojowska-Philp, *Full Bloom*, p. 112.
14. Lisle, *Portrait of an Artist*, p. 94.
15. Drohojowska-Philp, *Full Bloom*, p. 118.
16. Georgia O'Keeffe Exhibit, Panhandle-Plains Historical Museum, Canyon, Texas.
17. Drohojowska-Philp, *Full Bloom*, p. 119.
18. Lisle, *Portrait of an Artist*, p. 96.
19. Drohojowska-Philp, *Full Bloom*, p. 126.
20. Ibid., p. 122.
21. Lisle, *Portrait of an Artist*, pp. 105–106.
22. Drohojowska-Philp, *Full Bloom*, p. 133.
23. Ibid., p. 135.

24. Didion, *We Tell Ourselves Stories in Order to Live*, p. 274.
25. Drohojowska-Philp, *Full Bloom*, p. 144.
26. Lisle, *Portrait of an Artist*, p. 121.
27. Drohojowska-Philp, *Full Bloom*, p. 161.
28. Lisle, *Portrait of an Artist*, p. 131.
29. Drohojowska-Philp, *Full Bloom*, p. 162.
30. Eisler, *O'Keeffe & Stieglitz*, p. 186.
31. Lisle, *Portrait of an Artist*, p. 137.
32. Ibid.
33. Ibid., p. 135.
34. Ibid., pp. 137–138.

CHAPTER 5: DISCOVERING A NEW WAY OF SEEING

1. Drohojowska-Philp, *Full Bloom*, p. 194.
2. Ibid., p. 182.
3. Ibid., p. 195.
4. Ibid., p. 210.
5. Ibid.
6. Eisler, *O'Keeffe & Stieglitz*, p. 276.
7. Drohojowska-Philp, *Full Bloom*, p. 213.
8. Ibid., p. 211.
9. Didion, *We Tell Ourselves Stories in Order to Live*, p. 273.
10. Lisle, *Portrait of an Artist*, p. 147.
11. Ibid., p. 128.
12. Ibid.
13. Ibid., p. 129.
14. Eisler, *O'Keeffe & Stieglitz*, p. 321.
15. Benke, *Flowers in the Desert*, p. 31.
16. Lisle, *Portrait of an Artist*, p. 171.
17. Eisler, *O'Keeffe & Stieglitz*, pp. 327–328.
18. Lisle, *Portrait of an Artist*, p. 172.
19. Ibid.

20.   Benke, *Flowers in the Desert*, p. 32.
21.   Lisle, *Portrait of an Artist*, p. 173.
22.   Ibid., pp. 173–174.
23.   Ibid., p. 176.
24.   Benke, *Flowers in the Desert*, p. 40.
25.   Ibid., p. 52.
26.   Drohojowska-Philp, *Full Bloom*, p. 292.
27.   Ibid.

CHAPTER 6: FINDING HER TRUE HOME
1.   Ibid., p. 296.
2.   Lisle, *Portrait of an Artist*, p. 222.
3.   Ibid., p. 223.
4.   Ibid., p. 243.
5.   Drohojowska-Philp, *Full Bloom*, p. 319.
6.   Lisle, *Portrait of an Artist*, pp. 251–252.
7.   Drohojowska-Philp, *Full Bloom*, p. 332.
8.   Ibid.
9.   Lisle, *Portrait of an Artist*, p. 252.
10.   Ibid., p. 259.
11.   Ibid., p. 263.

CHAPTER 7: GHOST RANCH
1.   Ibid., p. 275.
2.   Drohojowska-Philp, *Full Bloom*, p. 361.
3.   Lisle, *Portrait of an Artist*, p. 297.
4.   Benke, *Flowers in the Desert*, p. 64.
5.   Lisle, *Portrait of an Artist*, p. 298.
6.   Ibid.
7.   Ibid., p. 299.
8.   Ibid.
9.   Ibid., p. 300.
10.   Ibid., p. 311.
11.   Ibid., p. 322.

CHAPTER 8: A WOMAN ON HER OWN

1. Ibid., p. 351.
2. Ibid., p. 364.
3. Ibid., p. 373.
4. Ibid., p. 376.
5. Ibid., p. 383.
6. Ibid.
7. Ibid., p. 387.
8. Benke, *Flowers in the Desert*, p. 83.

BIBLIOGRAPHY

Benke, Britta. *Georgia O'Keeffe 1887–1986: Flowers in the Desert*. New York: Barnes & Noble Books, 1994.

Didion, Joan. *We Tell Ourselves Stories in Order to Live: Collected Nonfiction*. New York: Everyman's Library, 2006.

Drohojowska-Philp, Hunter. *Full Bloom: The Art and Life of Georgia O'Keeffe*. New York: W.W. Norton & Company, 2004.

Eisler, Benita. *O'Keeffe & Stieglitz: An American Romance*. New York: Penguin Books, 1992.

Lisle, Laurie. *Portrait of an Artist: A Biography of Georgia O'Keeffe*. New York: Washington Square Press, 1981.

Pollitzer, Anita. *A Woman on Paper: Georgia O'Keeffe*. New York: Touchstone, 1988.

FURTHER RESOURCES

BOOKS

Dow, Arthur Wesley. *Composition: A Series of Exercises in Art Structure for the Use of Students and Teachers*. Berkeley, Calif.: University of California Press, 1998.

Kudlinski, Kathleen. *The Spirit Catchers: An Encounter with Georgia O'Keeffe*. New York: Watson-Guptil Publications, 2004.

Lynes, Barbara Buhler. *Georgia O'Keeffe Museum Collections*. New York: Harry N. Abrams Inc., 2007.

Poling-Kempes, Lesley. *Ghost Ranch*. Tucson, Ariz.: University of Arizona Press, 2005.

Poling-Kempes, Lesley. *Valley of Shining Stone: The Story of Abiquiú*. Tucson, Ariz.: University of Arizona Press, 1997.

WEB SITES

Artcyclopedia-Georgia O'Keeffe
http://www.artcylopedia.com/artists/okeeffe_georgia.html

Georgia O'Keeffe Museum
http://www.okeeffemuseum.org

PICTURE CREDITS

INDEX

A

Abiquiú, N.M.
  architecture series and, 104–106
  garden and diet at, 103
  home open to tourists, 84
  O'Keeffe in, 106
  purchase of house in, 103–104
Abstraction, Bowls, Twin Lakes, Conn. (Strand), 58
Amarillo, Texas, 40–41
An American Place (Stieglitz gallery), 86, 90–91
Armory Show (International Exhibition of Modern Art), 42
art career. *See* career in art
Art Institute of Chicago, 31, 100
Art Students League (NYC), 8, 33–35
awards. *See* honors

B

background
  ambition to be artist as child, 22
  birth, 15
  Chatham Episcopal Institute, 28–30
  childhood memories, 17–18, 19–20
  and immigrant family, 15–17
  private art classes, 21
  schooling, 23–24
Barker, Vergil, 73
Bement, Alon, 11–12, 38–39
Benke, Britta
  on flower paintings, 75
  on O'Keeffe and New York City, 80
  on O'Keeffe's art and personality, 13–14
  on *Summer Days*, 96
Black Abstraction (O'Keeffe), 79
Black Bird with Snow-Covered Red Hills, A (O'Keeffe), 101
Black Cross with Stars and Blue (O'Keeffe), 85
Blue and Green Music (O'Keeffe), 66
Blue Lines (O'Keeffe), 57
Blue Morning Glories, New Mexico (O'Keeffe), 94

bones, painting of, 86–88
Braque, Georges, 43

C

Canyon, Texas, 54–56
career in art
  advertising in Chicago and, 9, 11, 38
  breakthrough to, 44–46
  bright colors and, 44, 55
  charcoal works, 47–48
  frustration of leaving art school, 7–9
  reputation, 97–101, 105–106
  student in Chicago, 30–33
  student in New York, 33–35
  swift rise to prominence, 12
  See also critical reviews; exhibitions; mentors; Stieglitz, Alfred
Charlottesville, South Carolina, 41–43
Chase, William Merritt, 34–35
Chatham Episcopal Institute, 28–30
Columbia, South Carolina, 44–46
Covarrubias, Miguel, 77
Cow's Skull, Red, White and Blue (O'Keeffe), 87–88
Cow's Skull with White Calico Roses (O'Keeffe), 87
critical reviews
  on 1933 exhibition, 90–91
  on artist in transition, 82
  on From the Faraway, Nearby, 96
  on flower painting, 75
  negativity of, 97–98
  on1936 exhibition, 94–95
  psychoanalysis of work, 54–55
  in retrospective catalog (1943), 100
  on sexuality in paintings, 70, 73, 76
  on skull and flower paintings, 87–88
  on urban landscapes, 80

D

Dannenberg, George, 34
Didion, Joan

on *Evening Star* series, 59
on *Sky Above Clouds*, 12–13
Didion, Quintana, 12, 111
diseases, fear of, 17
Dole Pineapple Company commission, 98
Dow, Arthur Wesley, 38–39, 41–43
Drohojowska-Philp, Hunter, 58, 59–60, 87–88
Duchamp, Marcel, 42
Dutch Girl cleanser logo, 38

E
Eisler, Benita
    on Elizabeth May Willis, 29
    on O'Keeffe's liberation, 33
    on Sacred Heart Academy, 26–27
Evening Star series (O'Keeffe), 59
exhibitions
    An American Place retrospective (1932), 90–91
    Anderson Galleries (1923), 69–70
    Armory Show, 42
    Art Institute of Chicago (1943), 100
    art show in 1929, 80, 81
    dual exhibition with Stieglitz, 72–73
    Exhibition of Paintings and Drawings Showing the Later Tendencies in Art, 67
    first showing of art, 52–53
    first solo show, 57
    Ghost Ranch work (1937), 95–96
    Museum of Modern Art (1946), 100
    New Mexico work (1930), 85
    New York Ghost Ranch (1936), 94
    skull and flower paintings (1932), 88
    Worcester Art Museum (1960), 110–111

F
flowers, painting of, 72–76
Freud, Sigmund, 53–54

From the Faraway, Nearby (O'Keefe), 96

G
Georgia O'Keeffe Museum, 84
Ghost Ranch
    first visit to, 92–93
    paintings inspired by, 94–95
    Rancho de los Burros, 84, 96–97
    reputation at peak at, 97–101
Great Depression, 85

H
Hamilton, Juan, 113–114
health issues, 60, 79, 80, 90–91, 98
Hiroshige: Color Prints from the Collection of Frank Lloyd Wright, 32
honors
    American Academy of Arts and Letters, 111–112
    as feminist icon, 113
    honorary doctorate from William and Mary, 98
    Kelly Prize, 36
    Medal of Freedom, 113
    National Institute of Arts and Letters, 104
Horse's Skull with Pink Rose (O'Keeffe), 87
Horse's Skull with White Rose (O'Keeffe), 87

I
in her own words. *See* quotations from O'Keeffe
International Exhibition of Modern Art (Armory Show), 42
It Was Blue and Green (O'Keeffe), 110
It Was Yellow and Pink (O'Keeffe), 110

J
Jewell, Edward Alden, 85

K
Kahlo, Firda, 109
Kelly Prize, 36

L

Ladder to the Moon (O'Keeffe), 105–106
Lake George summers, 61, 82, 90
landscapes, urban, 76–77, 79–80
legacy, 114
Lisle, Laurie
    on Dow method, 39
    on *From the Faraway, Nearby*, 96
    on flower paintings, 75
    on Ida Totto O'Keeffe, 17, 19
    on New Mexico, 83–84
    on O'Keeffe as loner, 20
    on O'Keeffe's love of Texas, 40–41
    on photographic influences on O'Keeffe, 72
    on reputation of O'Keeffe, 98
    on Stieglitz family's acceptance of O'Keeffe, 61
    on Williamsburg, 25
Luhan, Mabel Dodge
    background of, 81
    O'Keeffe's avoidance of, 86
Luhan, Tony, 81, 83, 84

M

MacDonald-Wright, Stanton, 66
Macmahon, Arthur, 51–52
Mann, Sarah, 21
McBride, Henry, 54, 63–64, 73
mentors
    Alon Bement, 11–12, 38–39
    Arthur Wesley Dow, 41–43
    Elizabeth May Willis, 28–29
    William Merritt Chase, 34–35
    See also Stieglitz, Alfred
modern art, emergence of, 43–44
Mumford, Lewis, 63, 80, 94–95
Museum of Modern Art, 100
Music–Pink and Blue (O'Keeffe), 66

N

Norman, Dorothy, 86, 90
Nude Descending a Staircase (Duchamp), 42

O

O'Keeffe, Pierce (grandfather), 15–16

O'Keeffe, Anita (sister), 11
O'Keeffe, Catherine (sister), 90
O'Keeffe, Claudia (sister), 56, 58
O'Keeffe, Francis Calixtus (father), 15, 29, 52
O'Keeffe, Georgia Totto
    death of, 114
    independence of, 13–14, 20, 27–28
    lifestyle of, 104–108
    as model, 36
    oval stone and, 112
    photographs of, 10, 78, 89, 95
    physical appearance of, 27, 56
    rediscovery of, 110–111
    reputation of, 97–101, 105–106
    Strand and, 58–59, 60–61
    Toomer and, 91
    travels of, 98, 108–110
    See also Abiquiú, N.M.; background; career in art; health issues; honors; quotations from O'Keeffe; Stieglitz, Alfred; teaching career
O'Keeffe, Georgia Totto (works)
    Black Abstraction, 79
    Black Cross with Stars and Blue, 85
    Blue and Green Music, 66
    Blue Lines, 57
    Blue Morning Glories, New Mexico, 94
    Cow's Skull, Red, White and Blue, 87–88
    Cow's Skull with White Calico Roses, 87
    Evening Star series, 59
    Horse's Skull with Pink Rose, 87
    Horse's Skull with White Rose, 87
    Music–Pink and Blue, 66
    Purple Hills No. 11, 94
    Ram's Head, White Hollyhock–Hills, 94
    Red and Orange Streak, 66
    Shanty, The, 70
    Sheldon with Sunspots, The, 77
    Sky Above Clouds, 12–13
    Specials, 48, 54, 57
    Two Calla Lilies on Pink, 75
O'Keeffe, Ida (sister), 90

O'Keeffe, Ida Ten Eyck Totto
   (mother)
   art classes for Georgia
      arranged by, 21, 30
   death of, 52
   marriage of, 15–17
   tuberculosis of, 11, 52
   as woman of culture, 19–20
O'Keeffe, Kate (grandmother), 16

P
Palo Duro Canyon, 54–55
Peck, Arthur Newton, 93
Pelvis and Sky series (O'Keeffe),
   66
Pemberton, Murdock, 81
Phillips, Duncan, 70
Picasso, Pablo, 43
Pollitzer, Aline, 51–52
Pollitzer, Anita, 42, 44, 49–50
Pollitzer, Sigmund, 51
Porter, Eliot, 112
Purple Hills No. 11 (O'Keeffe), 94

Q
quotations from O'Keeffe
   on artistic breakthrough, 47
   on being afraid, 56
   on "dirty painting," 70
   on first showing of her art, 53
   on first twelve years, 25
   on flowers, 73
   on inspiration for Black
      Abstraction, 79
   letter to Stieglitz, 50–51
   on looking at paintings, 9
   on painting as way of expres-
      sion, 23
   on painting skulls, 88
   on painting the desert, 86
   on singing, 35
   on teaching art, 55
   on Texas, 40, 55
   on unhappiness in Canyon, 60
   on walks with Claudia, 59
   on women artists, 67

R
Radio City Music Hall, 90
Ram's Head, White Hollyhock–Hills
   (O'Keeffe), 94
Rancho de los Burros, 96–97

Ranchos de Taos (Ghost Ranch),
   84, 85
realism, rejection of, 8–9
Red and Orange Streak (O'Keeffe),
   66
Reid, Ted, 60
reviews, critical. See critical
   reviews
Rich, Daniel Catton, 100
Rosenfeld, Paul, 70
Rousseau, Henri, 43

S
Schwartz, Sanford, on photographs of O'Keeffe, 63
sexuality in paintings, 73, 76
Shanty, The (O'Keeffe), 70
Sheldon with Sunspots, The
   (O'Keeffe), 77
Sky Above Clouds (O'Keeffe),
   12–13, 111
Specials (O'Keeffe), 48, 54, 57
Speicher, Eugene, 36
Spring (O'Keeffe), 104, 105
Stieglitz, Alfred
   291 gallery of, 43
   concept of equivalents and,
      71–72
   death of, 100
   deterioration of personal rela-
      tionship with O'Keeffe, 86
   divorce and remarriage to
      O'Keeffe, 71
   infatuation with O'Keeffe, 60
   as judge of portrait of
      O'Keeffe, 36
   as lover and caretaker of
      O'Keeffe, 61
   marriage to O'Keeffe, 71
   as married man, 58
   as mentor to O'Keeffe, 52–53
   Norman and, 86, 90, 102
   O'Keefe's tribute to, 100–101
   O'Keeffe's admiration of,
      43–44, 45, 51
   O'Keeffe's mourning of,
      102–103
   photographs of O'Keeffe by,
      62–63, 65
   profile portrait of, 37
   response to O'Keefe's draw-
      ings, 50–51

Strand, Beck, 82, 83
Strand, Paul, 58–60, 82
Summer Days (O'Keeffe), 95–96

T
Taos, New Mexico, 81–83, 85
teaching career
    Amarillo, Tex., 40–41
    Charlottesville, S. C., 41–43
    Columbia, S.C., 44–46
Toomer, Jean, 91
Totto, George Victor (grandfather), 16
Totto, Isabel Wyckoff (grandmother), 16
Two Calla Lilies on Pink (O'Keeffe), 75

U
urban landscapes, 76–77, 79–80

V
Vanderpoel, John, 32

W
White Album, The (Didion), 12
Williamsburg, Virginia, move to, 23–25, 33
Willis, Elizabeth May, 28–29, 33
Wilson, Edmund, 75
women, as artists, 8, 67–69, 76
Wright, Frank Lloyd, 32
Wright, Willard H., 54

ABOUT THE AUTHOR

DENNIS ABRAMS attended Antioch College, where he majored in English and communications. A voracious reader since the age of three, Dennis is a freelance writer who has written numerous books for young-adult readers, including biographies of Hamid Karzai, Ty Cobb, Anthony Horowitz, Xerxes, Rachael Ray, and Hillary Rodham Clinton. He lives in Houston, Texas, with his partner of 20 years, two cats, and their dog, Junie B.